TEACH YOURS

CW00602604

C H O

ENSION

CHOOSING A PENSION

Leo Gough

TEACH YOURSELF BOOKS

Disclaimer

This book is intended only as a general guide to choosing a pension. It is suggested that individuals should seek professional advice about their pensions. While every effort has been made to ensure accuracy, no legal responsibility or liability can be accepted by the author or the Publisher for any errors or omissions.

Note that many figures quoted refer to 1995/96 rates, and may change in subsequent years.

British Library Cataloguing in Publication Data

Gough, Leo
   Choosing a pension. – (Teach Yourself)
   1. Pensions 2. Saving and investment 3. Retirement income
   I. Title
   331.2'52

ISBN 0 340 670010

First published 1996
Impression number 10 9 8 7 6 5 4 3 2 1
Year   1999 1998 1997 1996

The 'Teach Yourself' name and logo are registered trade marks of
Hodder & Stoughton Ltd in the UK.

Typeset by Transet Limited, Coventry, England.
Printed in Great Britain for Hodder & Stoughton Educational, a division of Hodder Headline Plc, 338 Euston Road, London NW1 3BH by Cox & Wyman Limited, Reading, Berks.

CONTENTS

1

WHAT IS A PENSION?

We are in the middle of a quiet revolution. Not too many years ago, if you had a job, you could expect to keep it for life. Pensions were arranged accordingly. Now, most large employers are going through a phase of 'business process re-engineering', which is a fancy way of saying that employers are adapting to information technology, cutting their staff and encouraging people to work from home, using computers. Not many people these days can expect to spend their whole lives in one job; you will probably have at least two or three new employers during your working life, and many more people are becoming self-employed, working on short-term contracts. In addition, more women are working.

These changes mean that the pension system is changing too. The rules are getting more complicated, and while you have more freedom in your pension arrangements than ever before, you will need to pay for independent advice to make sure that you make the right decisions. This book is designed to help you do this, so that you can enjoy a prosperous retirement.

What is a pension?

Pensions were invented to protect people from poverty in old age. The basic principle is simple; pensions are a way of saving money out of your income (combined with a state subsidy and, for employees, an employer's contribution), so that you will have enough money to live on when you retire.

The government wants you to make proper pension arrangements, so it gives you tax concessions on your pension savings. The younger you are when you start a pension, the more time the money has to grow, and the tax advantages help this enormously.

Why bother with a pension?

Many people go through life without ever thinking of the future. No one can say that this is wrong, as long as you appreciate what may happen once you have become old and unable to work.

There are a great many powerful reasons why you should invest in pensions. As you can see from the table below, pensions grow much faster than a building society deposit.

The cumulative value of a pension fund

This shows the cost of delaying the time you start making pension contributions, based on making a contribution of £1,000 a year at 4 different ages.

Age when payment started	Accumulated value of the fund at age 65
44 years 11 months	£145,607
49 years 11 months	£76,545
54 years 11 months	£32,200
59 years 11 months	£9,223

Source: Equitable Life Assurance Society

You might think that if you delayed the time you started a pension by 5 years it would simply reduce the value of the pension fund by £5,000 plus 5 years' loss of interest, but you have also lost the benefit of having the funds growing tax free over the whole time you are saving. Thus, if you started contributing at 45 rather than at 50, you would create an extra £70,000 (roughly) by the time you reached the male retirement age of 65.

If you are going to save money until you retire, it makes sense to do it through the tax-efficient means of a pension. All the money you put in receives full tax relief at either 25 per cent or 40 per cent. It then grows completely free of all tax. When you come to retire you can take a large proportion of the fund as a tax-free cash sum. The pension income itself is taxable, however.

When should you start your pension?

You can't start a pension too soon; the longer you wait before starting, the less you will get out when you retire. It is a good idea to have started by the time you are 30. Younger people, and people with families, may need all the money that they are earning now, so if you are in this position, don't be too worried – the world isn't going to come to an end if you start your pension a little later in life.

Aren't there other ways of saving for retirement?

Although pensions are very tax efficient, they are not the only way to save for retirement. Your real objective should be to accumulate as large an amount of capital as possible by the time you retire from work, so that you can receive as much income as possible after you retire. The tax advantages of pensions over other forms of savings (see Chapter 8) give pension contributions a head start, but pensions have some disadvantages:

- Pension contributions are effectively 'locked in'. You can't usually withdraw any money before your retirement age.
- When you retire, only about a quarter of the pension fund can be taken out as cash. The rest of the fund has to be taken as income.
- The pension income stops when you, or in some cases your spouse, dies; this is different from a capital sum which you have saved in some other way, because in the latter case you can leave the money to your children or others when you die.
- There are limits to the amount you can contribute to a pension fund – broadly, 15 per cent of your income if you are an employee, and 17.5–40 per cent if you are self-employed, subject to your age and overall 'capping'. Only 1 in 10 people actually contribute the maximum over their working lives – the average contribution is about 5 per cent, a third of the maximum.

Applying the principle of not putting all your eggs in one basket, there is a good argument for not relying solely on your pension; savings schemes over which you have more control, such as PEPs and TESSAs, may also be worth having. If you own your own home, you could consider moving to a smaller place once the children have grown up and you have retired – this, too, can give you tax-free cash for your retirement.

Figure 1.1 Pensions and your life stages

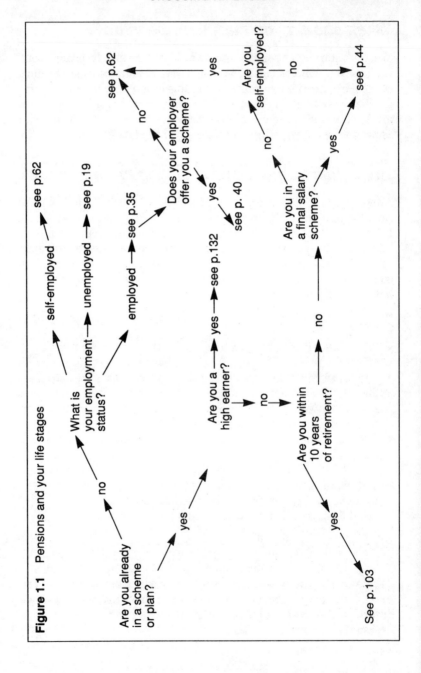

Life-stage decisions

At different times of your life, you will have to make decisions about your pension arrangements. On page 4 is a chart to help you find where particular issues are covered in this book:

How does inflation affect pensions?

What you really need from a pension is money that you can spend in real terms. It is no good having pension income of £1,000 per month if that is the price of a cup of tea a few years after you have retired! What you need is £1,000 per month in real terms – in other words, you need an income that is protected against inflation.

Unfortunately, no one knows exactly what future rates of inflation will be. It is all based on estimates. Life assurance companies often project forward at rates of 6 per cent and 12 per cent growth. This produces astronomical pension figures for young people, so it is confusing if you are told that paying in £50 a month will produce a pension of £100,000 in 30 years' time. If inflation were to average 7 per cent per year for the next 30 years, then £100,000 would be worth only £12,277 in today's terms.

Ask your plan provider to give you figures based on a 'real' rate of return of, say, 3 per cent or 4 per cent. This means that you are assuming that your pension fund will grow at 3 per cent or 4 per cent more than inflation, rather than 6 per cent or 12 per cent. This will give you a better idea of what you should contribute to get an adequate pension.

Preparing for retirement

If you are coming up to retirement, it is worth going on a course or joining a society. You will need to think about other things as well as money – your health, housing, and lifestyle, for example.

The Pre-Retirement Association is a charity which helps people to get good advice on all these matters at low cost. Their address is listed at the back of this book.

Getting to grips with the pension rules

There is no doubt about it – pensions are complicated! Don't despair, though. If you take the trouble, you will be able to get a good grasp of how they work, although you will need professional advice as well. Even though not all the information in this book will be directly relevant to your situation at the moment, it is worth reading it all the way through. If you do so, you will get a sense of the overall picture, which will help you plan if your circumstances change in the future.

2

CHOOSING A PENSION

— The different kinds of pension —

There are four main kinds of pension arrangement:

- The basic state pension
- The State Earnings Related Pension Scheme (SERPS)
- Occupational pension schemes
- Personal pension plans.

You can't be in all four kinds at the same time, but most people will find that they will collect entitlements to more than one type during their working lives. Of the four, the most important in terms of their monetary value, are occupational pension schemes (for employees only) and personal pension plans. We will look at all four types in great detail later in this book, but for now you should appreciate that:

- With one exception (see page 65) you can't, if you are a member of an occupational scheme, take out a personal pension as well.
- If you already have a personal pension plan and you want to join an occupational scheme, you must stop contributing to your personal plan.

In general, such changes don't mean that you actually lose what you have already paid into a scheme.

It is not unusual to change your employment status several times during your career; at one time you might be an employee in an occupational scheme, at another you might be employed by a company which has no pension provision and at other times you might be self-employed and ineligible for occupational pension schemes.

If this happens, you will end up with a collection of small pensions of different types, and you will need to keep track of them all.

Remember to keep in touch with old pension schemes and plan providers. If you move house or change your name you should contact all the schemes and providers to give them your new name and address. Sometimes schemes are taken over by new administrators – if you are notified of this, you should contact them to make sure they have all your details and entitlements correctly recorded.

What pensions am I eligible for?

Apart from the basic state pension, which almost everyone will be able to claim, the pension(s) you are eligible for depend on whether you are employed or self-employed.

Keeping proper records

From the time that you start your first pension scheme, you will receive a great deal of paperwork. It is important to get into the habit of keeping all these documents safe and properly organised. You should also keep copies of any letters that you write, and notes of telephone calls that you make regarding your pensions. If you do this, it will be much easier to assert your rights and stop any mistakes occurring.

How much of a pension income will I need?

Whatever type of pension scheme you are in, it is worth doing some sums to see what kind of pension you are likely to get in retirement. When retirement is 30 years away, this estimate won't be very accurate, but it is still worth doing.

First, work out what sort of pension you are likely to get, given your current arrangements:

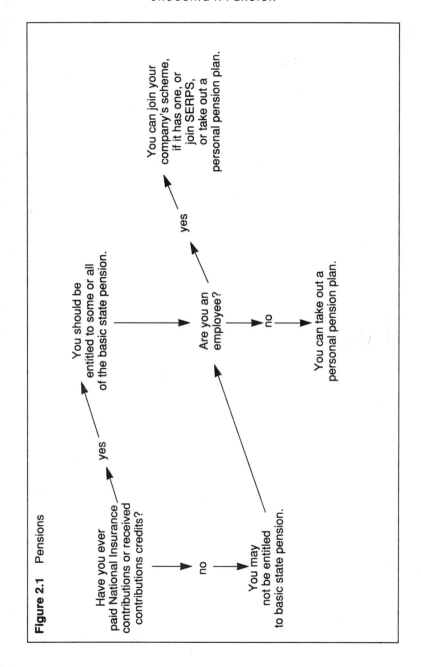

Figure 2.1 Pensions

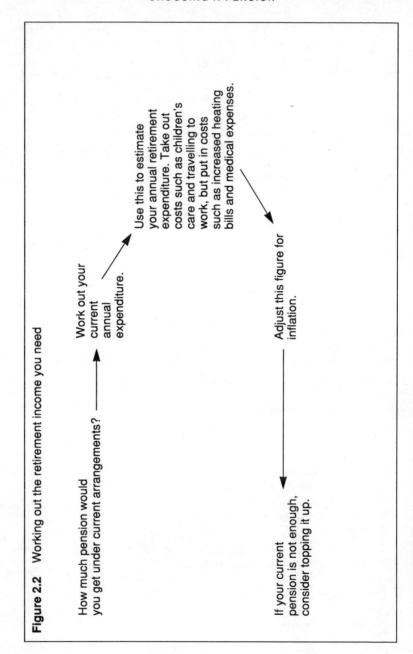

Figure 2.2 Working out the retirement income you need

Next, work out how much you would need to live on, in today's money, if you were retired. If you say, 'As much as possible', you are giving the right answer. It's easy to underestimate how much you will need in retirement, especially in the later years – old people need to have fun too!

To estimate the income you will need when you retire, look at your present annual expenditure. Make list of all the items, like this:

1   accommodation (mortgage or rent)
2   food (including meals in restaurants and cafés, school dinners, snacks, etc.
3   household consumables
    (things you buy for the house and garden, such as detergents, weedkiller and hoover bags)
4   bills:
    • telephone
    • electricity
    • gas
    • oil
    • solid fuel
    • council tax
    • water rates
    • TV licence
    • equipment rental and HP
5   insurance:
    • buildings insurance
    • contents insurance
6   car:
    • car insurance
    • fuel
    • repairs and servicing
    • road tax and MOT
    • loss of value ('depreciation')
    • AA/RAC membership
7   other transport
    (including trains, buses and taxis)
8   savings and investment payments
    • TESSA
    • PEPS
    • bank/building society deposits
    • SAYE

- life assurance
- pension contributions
- other
9 house maintenance
10 holiday
- travel
- hotels
- spending money
11 other personal items
- cigarettes
- alcohol (include what you spend in pubs)
- theatre/cinema/video
- sports and hobbies
- newspapers, magazines, audio cassettes
- clothes
- other
12 miscellaneous
- furniture
- pet food and vet fees
- borrowings
- other
- bank interest and charges
13 tax and National Insurance.

Total expenditure: £ _____

Now, imagine that you are a pensioner, with all the special concessions that pensioners get on travel, prescriptions and so on, and make out a new list. Delete the items you won't be spending on after retirement – these may include:

- mortgage payments – if you will have paid off your mortgage by the time you retire
- National Insurance – you won't have to pay this once you have stopped working
- the cost of travelling to work
- your pension contributions
- the cost of bringing up children.

You may need to add some items, such as medical insurance, and increased heating costs. Add up the total, remembering that pension income is taxable at the normal rates. This gives you an estimate of how much income you will need in today's money. If you are using a professional pensions adviser, he or she will help you make these estimates. Remember, though, that they are only estimates, and the further away from retirement you are, the less realistic they will be.

So, follow the simple steps below and you should reach a reasonable funding figure for your pension.

1 Decide what your target pension is in today's money – for example, £14,000.
2 Have your adviser work out what this figure will be when you retire, based on your view of inflation.
3 Have your adviser work out how much your current pension arrangements will be worth as retirement income.
4 If there is a difference between 1 and 2, you will need to top up your pension. Ask your adviser for a quotation that will produce a pension of the inflated size, assuming that the pension fund increases in value, through sound investment, at a rate of 3 per cent or 4 per cent above your chosen inflation figure.

——— Getting financial advice ———

Throughout this book you will be encouraged to get professional advice before making any big decision regarding your pension. In this section we will look at the different types of adviser, and how to get the most out of them.

The Financial Services Act, which came into effect in 1986, has introduced a great deal of protection for the consumer. The system is based on a number of Self-Regulating Organisations (SROs) and Recognised Professional Bodies (RPBs). SROs and RPBs regulate all the different types of people you can go to for advice on money matters.

● RPBs include the Law Society, which governs solicitors, and the Institute of Chartered Accountants.
● SROs include FIMBRA, regulating independent financial advisers and LAUTRO, which regulates insurance companies and unit trust companies. The Personal Investment Authority (PIA) is taking over from FIMBRA and LAUTRO.

Only ever go for professional advice to someone who is a member of an SRO or an RPB – this is your first line of defence should anything go wrong.

The range of financial advisers

The range is very wide, partly because no single adviser can be an expert in all financial matters, and partly because there is a good deal of money to be made out of giving advice. The fact that an adviser makes money should not deter you – if the advice is really good, it will be worth the cost. Not every adviser is really good, though; some are little more than inexperienced salesmen with not much training.

Since there are so many specialist advisers, it is a good idea to develop an ongoing relationship with several different ones. This way, you can build up a better picture of the overall approach to take, and benefit from their different areas of expertise.

Here are some of the main advisers you are likely to encounter:

Tied agents

Tied agents represent a company, most often an insurance company, and sell only the products offered by that company. They don't have to tell you how much commission they are making, but they do have to tell you that they are tied. High street banks and most building societies are tied agents. Tied agents are backed by large companies, so they are unlikely to go bust, and they may, sometimes, be able to give you the best deal on a particular product. Never sign an agreement that includes a penalty clause where you have to pay a tied agent a sum of money if you allow an insurance policy or a mortgage to lapse.

Independent financial advisers (IFAs)

These are people who may or may not have an impressive set of qualifications; the only professional qualification that they must have is the Financial Planning Certificate. IFAs have to tell you all about their charges and commissions, and must give you the best independent advice they can. IFAs may either charge you a fee for their advice, or take a commission from the company from which you purchase a product. If you pay a fee, ask the adviser to rebate any commissions to you.

Accountants

Not all accountants will give advice, but those that do are IFAs. Their great area of expertise is usually taxation, but check their qualifications and experience closely. Experienced accountants may know a great deal about business in general.

Solicitors

These will also be IFAs. Their area of expertise will be in certain aspects of the law, and you should try to find out which aspects these are. As a rule they are a cautious breed and don't necessarily know much about business. They have a tendency to charge highly for their time, and they tend to take a lot of time.

Bank managers

Gone are the days of the wise old bank manager who knew all the bank's customers intimately. Nowadays, you are more likely to find that your 'personal account manager' changes every year or two. Bank managers are tied agents and under pressure to sell you a host of financial products. Their area of expertise is in lending and cash flow; if you are thinking of borrowing, it is worth hearing what they have to say, even if you go somewhere else to borrow.

Building society managers

Most of these are tied. Building societies are becoming more like banks every day. Their area of expertise is mortgages.

Insurance company representatives

These are tied. They should know their own products backwards and be able to explain what is a complicated subject clearly. Don't sign up for anything without getting opinions from other kinds of adviser first.

Insurance brokers

These may be tied or independent. The good ones know a great deal about the ins and outs of different insurance companies, and, even more importantly, how to make sure that the companies actually pay out if you claim, which depends on the wording of the policy and the information that you give when you take the policy out.

Dealing with an adviser

Although a tied agent may give you good advice, in many cases it would be better to go to an IFA and pay for your advice with a fixed fee. This is because a good IFA will know the whole market well and be able to give you an objective analysis of your choices and their pros and cons.

One of the first things an adviser has to do is to conduct a 'fact-find'. This means that you will be asked to answer a large number of detailed questions about your circumstances and finances. It is in your interests to answer these questions fully, since any advice you get will be based on your answers.

The adviser will want to know:

- your age and sex
- your employment status
- your income
- the tax you pay
- your state of health
- if you are married
- details about your children
- your regular financial commitments such as your mortgage payments and household bills
- what you think your expenditure will be after you have retired
- when you want to retire
- how much you expect from state pensions
- details of any occupational scheme you can join
- details of any previous occupational schemes you have belonged to
- details of any personal plans
- details of any current life insurance
- details of any other savings or investments
- your attitude towards investment risk
- any likely changes to any of the above.

The 'hard sell'

Although agents and advisers are strictly controlled, you may still be approached at home as the result of a 'cold call'.

If this happens, the salesman must:

- make clear what company he or she represents, and give you a business card;
- respect your wishes and end the call if you don't want the salesman to continue;
- send you a cancellation notice which gives you 14 days within which you can back out of the deal, if you sign up for any product.

In general, it is not a good idea to sign up for anything without first having familiarised yourself with all your options and having given yourself plenty of time to think. Pensions are long-term commitments, so don't make any hasty decisions that you may regret later.

Questions to ask your advisers

These may seem extremely cheeky questions, but it is your money, and you have every right to ask them. Try to get the answers to all of these in writing.

1 Are you an independent adviser or are you tied?
2 Which regulatory body are you authorised by? Are you fully authorised?
3 Will you refer me to satisfied customers who I can ask about the quality of your service?
4 Do you have professional indemnity insurance? With what company? (This insurance will pay out claims if you have to sue the adviser for some reason.)
5 How long have you worked in the advice industry and which companies have you worked for in the last ten years?
6 What is your conduct record with your regulatory body? Have you ever been interviewed by them on disciplinary matters?
7 Are you an agent for any financial service company, and if so, who?
8 What will be your commission, if any, on the transactions you advise?
9 What are your charges in detail?
10 What is the risk to my money?
11 Why are you advising me to do these things?
12 Are you authorised to handle my cash, or do my cheques have to be made out to the company which I buy the financial product from? (The latter is probably safer, even if the adviser is authorised to handle cash).

Conclusion

In an ideal world you would develop long-term relationships with two or three advisers in different fields, and conduct regular reviews with them – say, every year or two, and whenever your circumstances changed significantly. If you are fortunate enough to find advisers with whom you can do this, you will have a battery of experience and financial wisdom on your side. Achieving such relationships takes effort, good judgement and time – they are like marriages, and shouldn't usually be rushed. In the meantime, take things slowly and don't sign up for long-term commitments without taking the trouble to:

- think them over carefully
- read up on them in the financial press
- discuss them with more experienced friends and relatives
- and make sure you understand your choices.

Remember, the more effort you put in to understanding your finances, the more your advisers will be able to help you.

3
THE BASIC
STATE PENSION

Not too many years ago older people would warn you of the crucial importance of having a full National Insurance contribution record – 'If you don't have that,' people would say, 'you won't have any protection for your old age, because you won't get the full state pension.' However, the situation is changing rapidly.

The United Kingdom has one of the most, if not *the* most, complicated pension systems in Europe, and it will be getting even more complicated over the next 20 years or so. If you were cynical, you might even say that it is intentionally designed to be overcomplicated. At the same time, UK state pensions are lower than in most other European countries and are falling behind even more. From the point of view of the public, the state pension scheme is subject to the 'law of diminishing returns' – in other words, it requires more and more effort to get less and less out of it.

In spite of this, you shouldn't ignore the value of the state pensions as a part of your overall retirement income. We can't simply assume, as people could in the post-war period, that the basic state pension will be enough to live on when we have retired. It is barely enough to live on now, and it certainly won't be in the future.

Entitlement

Almost everyone in the United Kingdom can claim the basic state pension when they reach the age of 60 for women or 65 for men. The

Figure 3.1 The basic state pension – a quick guide

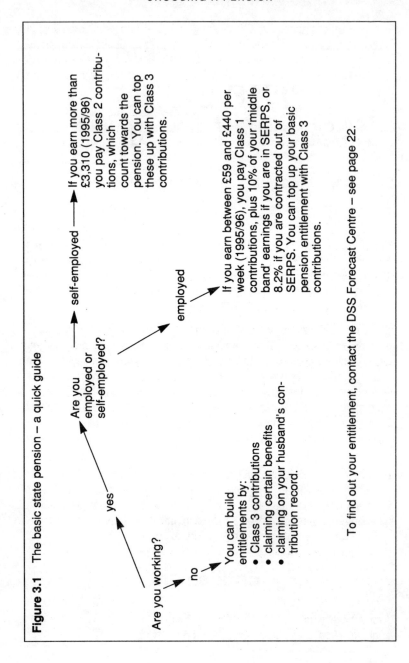

Are you working?

no → You can build entitlements by:
• Class 3 contributions
• claiming certain benefits
• claiming on your husband's contribution record.

yes → Are you employed or self-employed?

self-employed → If you earn more than £3,310 (1995/96) you pay Class 2 contributions, which count towards the pension. You can top these up with Class 3 contributions.

employed → If you earn between £59 and £440 per week (1995/96), you pay Class 1 contributions, plus 10% of your 'middle band' earnings if you are in SERPS, or 8.2% if you are contracted out of SERPS. You can top up your basic pension entitlement with Class 3 contributions.

To find out your entitlement, contact the DSS Forecast Centre – see page 22.

weekly level of pension in 1995/96 is £59.15 with an additional £35.30 for a wife claiming the pension on the basis of her husband's National Insurance contribution record. Whether or not you will receive the full amount of the basic state pension depends on your National Insurance contribution record.

Every year, the amount of pension is increased in line with the Retail Prices Index, which is a measure of inflation. The pension counts as taxable income and you must declare it on your tax return.

Common difficulties with the pension

If you left school at 16 and were in full-time employment until you retired at the state retirement age, you won't have much trouble with your pension rights. However, most people these days don't have such straightforward careers – we change our jobs, drop in and out of company pension schemes, leave work to bring up children and then return to work, and do many other things that have an effect on our entitlement.

Here are some common difficulties that you may encounter:

● The state retirement age for women is likely to be raised in about 2020, which may cause some difficulties for women who are currently in their early 40s (see below).
● Many company schemes are 'integrated', which means that the scheme takes the basic state pension into account in setting the company pension; this can adversely affect lower earners and people who are not eligible for a state pension (see Chapter 4, page 46).
● More people are retiring early, which affects how much state pension they will get.

Women's state retirement age

At present, women's state retirement age is 60. Once you have reached this age you can claim the state pension, but, just as importantly, you can also get many other kinds of benefits such as cheaper travel. In 1993 the government announced that it would introduce equal pension ages for men and women by 2020, raising the retirement age for women to 65. As yet, the full details of how this will be phased in are not known, but if you were born after April 1955 you can expect your state retirement age to be 65.

If you are a woman who was born between April 1950 and April 1955 you will be affected by the phasing-in of the new retirement age, and will have a retirement age somewhere between 60 and 65, depending on your date of birth.

How much basic state pension will I get?

You can't know for certain, any more than you can know when you will die. What you can do, though, is get a pensions forecast from the DSS from time to time which will help you with your pension planning.

To apply for a forecast, get form BR19 from your local DSS office and send it to the Retirement Pensions Forecast and Advisory service (RPFA), whose address is on the form. After a few weeks they will send you details of:

- how much basic pension you have built up so far;
- how much pension you will get if your employment circumstances don't change until you retire;
- things you can do to increase the amount of pension you will get if you are not eligible for the full amount.

You are entitled to one free forecast each year. Take advantage of this – it is the most straightforward and practical way of monitoring your entitlement.

Who gets the full amount of basic state pension?

Whether or not you will receive the full amount of the basic state pension depends on your National Insurance contribution record.

Your entitlement to this pension can be gained in one of three main ways:

1 The most common way is by the payment of National Insurance contributions, either Class 1 (for employees), Class 2 (for the self-employed) or Class 3 (voluntary contributions from people who want to build up their entitlement but do not pay either Class 1 or Class 2 contributions).

2 You may be able to get contribution credits if you have been receiving unemployment benefit, sickness benefit, invalidity pension, severe disablement allowance or payments for approved training. If so, you will be treated as if you actually had paid sufficient National Insurance contributions.

3 A married woman may be able to claim a reduced level of basic state pension on the basis of National Insurance contributions paid by her husband (see page 31).

The pension is taxable, but it is not means tested, so you need not worry about the effect of having other savings, and it is not affected even if you are receiving other social security benefits.

National Insurance (NI)

Despite its name, National Insurance is not insurance at all – the money you contribute is not invested for you, but is paid out directly to others; there is no real guarantee, if you are young now, that you will receive benefits in old age because of your contributions during your working life. This is an area of significant concern at the moment because the United Kingdom, like most other developed countries, has an 'ageing population', which means that people are living longer than they used to, and relatively few children are being born; this trend, which is likely to continue, may result in massive numbers of pensioners being supported by a small number of working people in the next century. How this is going to be handled is anybody's guess, but the present system will inevitably be adjusted, and some people may suffer. National Insurance contributions are in practice a kind of taxation on the income of employees, the self-employed and employers.

National Insurance contributions are not officially called a tax, and the rates are proposed to Parliament by the Secretary of State for Social Security rather than the Chancellor of the Exchequer. In reality, however, National Insurance contributions are indeed a tax; they must be paid by the employed and the self-employed (where earnings exceed a certain level) and by employers. Almost all National Insurance contributions are collected with income tax and then paid by the Inland Revenue to the Department of Social Security. The DSS receives some contributions direct.

A small proportion of the total contributions received by the DSS is passed to the National Health Service Account and the rest is paid to the National Insurance Fund. In addition to pensions, the other major state social security benefits such as widows' benefits, unemployment and invalidity benefits are paid from the National Insurance Fund.

The classes of National Insurance

The 'classes', or categories, of National Insurance are levied on different kinds of income, but never on investment income or pension schemes. The classes are:

Class 1

This relates to employees. It is divided into primary Class 1 NI, which is paid by you as the employee, and secondary Class 1 NI, which is paid by your employer. The rate of contribution is a percentage of what you earn.

Class 2

This is a flat-rate NI payment paid if you are self-employed, unless you have very low profits.

Class 3

These are voluntary contributions which may be paid if you want to maintain or improve your rights to certain state benefits.

Class 4

This class is also payable by the self-employed, as a percentage of all profits between a lower and an upper limit.

National Insurance contributions in 1995/96

Class 1	Weekly	Monthly	Yearly
Lower earnings limited	£59	£255.678	£3,068
Upper earnings limit	£440	£1,906.67	£22,880

Your contributions as an employee

Earnings	Contracted in to SERPS	Contracted out of SERPS
£59–£440 per week	2% on first £59 plus 10% on earnings between £59 and £440	2% on first £59 plus 8.2% on earnings between £59 and £440

Some widows and married women pay a lower rate.

Class 2 (Self-employed)
Earnings over £3,310 per annum   £5.85 a week

Class 3 (voluntary)   £5.75 per week

Class 4 (self-employed, additional levy)
Profits between £6,640 and £22,880 per annum   7.3%

Employees contracted in to SERPS

If you are contracted in to SERPS (see Chapter 3) you should note, if you have more earnings than the lower earnings limit, you pay National Insurance at 2 per cent of the first £59 per week of your earnings and 10 per cent of your earnings more than this. There is also an 'upper earnings level' – no one pays National Insurance on earnings they have over £440 a week or £22,880 a year (1995/96 figures).

Example for lower earners

Suppose you are employed and contracted in to SERPS, and you earn £6,000 a year. How much Class 1 National Insurance will you pay in the 1995/96 tax year?

2% of the first £3,068 = £61.36
10% of £2,932 = £293.20
Total earned income = £6,000   £354.56 = total Class 1 contributions

Example for higher earners

Suppose you are employed and contracted in to SERPS, and you earn £30,000 a year. How much Class 1 National Insurance will you pay in the 1995/96 tax year?

$$
\begin{aligned}
2\% \text{ of the first } £3,068 &= £61.36 \\
10\% \text{ of the balance of } £19,812 &= £1,981.20 \\
\text{(up to the upper earnings limit)} \\
0\% \text{ on } £7,120 &= 0 \\
\text{(over the upper earnings limit)} \\
\text{Total earned income} &= £30,000 \\
£2,042.56 &= \text{total Class 1 contributions}
\end{aligned}
$$

Employees who are contracted out of SERPS

If you are an employee who has decided to contract out of SERPS by using an appropriate personal pension (APP), then the amount of Class 1 contributions you pay will be exactly the same; the Department of Social Security (DSS) calculates the amount of your rebate annually and sends that amount to the APP provider (usually an insurance company) which you have chosen.

If you are an employee who has contracted out of SERPS because of a decision by your employer, through an occupational pension scheme, you will pay a reduced level of National Insurance on your earnings between the lower and upper earnings limits; these are known as your middle-band earnings (MEB).

This reduction is currently at 1.8 per cent, which makes the normal Class 1 rate of National Insurance 8.2 per cent. Note that earnings below £440 per week are still liable to National Insurance at 2 per cent unless your total earnings are below £59 per week, in which case you will pay no National Insurance, and earnings over the upper earnings limit are not liable to further National Insurance.

More on Class 1 National Insurance

This is paid by all employees who have salaries more than a 'lower earnings level' (LEL), which in 1995/96 is £59 per week or £3,068 per year. The level increases each year in line with inflation.

Paying this class of National Insurance qualifies you for state benefits, in particular.

- basic old age pension,
- possibly SERPS (see page 35)
- sickness benefits.

No National Insurance contributions are paid if your earnings are lower than the lower earnings limit.

How Class 1 contributions are collected

Primary Class 1 contributions (the ones that you, the employee, make) are collected by your employer and paid monthly to the local collector of taxes together with the secondary Class 1 contributions (the ones that your employer makes on your behalf). The Inland Revenue then pays this to the DSS.

Class 2 and Class 4 National Insurance

These are paid by people who are self-employed:

- Class 2 National Insurance is a flat-rate weekly payment (£5.85 in 1995/96) which must be paid by all self-employed people who earn more than the lower limit (£3,310 in 1995/96).
- Class 4 National Insurance is paid on profits over £6,640 in 1995/96; it is 7.3 per cent of your profits between the lower limit of £6,640 and an upper limit of £22,880 in 1995/96.
- Half of any Class 4 contributions you make are allowable against your income tax.

Example for lower earners

Suppose you are self-employed and earned £4,000 in profits in 1995/96.

Class 2 contributions are £5.85 per week. This is all you pay.

Example for higher earners

Suppose you are self-employed and earned £12,000 in profits in 1995/96. How much National Insurance contributions must you make in this year?

Class 2 contributions are £5.85 per week.

To calculate Class 4 contributions, subtract the lower Class 4 limit from your profits:

£12,000 – £6,640 = £5,360
7.3% of £5,360 is £391.28.

You pay £5.85 per week Class 2 contributions and £391.28 for the year's Class 4 contributions.

Example for even higher earners

Suppose you are self-employed and earning £42,000 in profits in 1995/96. How much National Insurance contributions must you make?

Class 2 contributions are £5.85 per week

To calculate Class 4 contributions, subtract the lower Class 4 limit from the upper Class 4 limit:

£22,880 – £6,640 = £16,240
7.3% of £16,240 is £1,185.52

You will pay £5.85 per week Class 2 contributions and £1,185.52 for the year's Class 4 contributions.

Class 3 National Insurance

Class 3 contributions can be made by anyone who is not paying either Class 1 or Class 2 contributions because their income is below the level at which you pay those classes. It is a flat rate of £5.75 per week in 1995/96.

———— Qualifying years ————

The percentage of the basic state pension you get depends on how many 'qualifying years' of National Insurance contributions you have. They are usually, but not always, tax years in which you have paid sufficient National Insurance contributions.

If you have paid a combination of different classes of contributions in a particular year you may still have built up a qualifying year.

If you have paid some contributions in a particular year, but not enough to make it a 'qualifying year', these contributions will not count towards your state pension entitlement – thus, they are a tax.

Which benefits count towards qualifying years?

The following benefits may all count towards your National Insurance contribution record, depending on your circumstances:

- unemployment benefit
- maternity benefit
- sickness benefits
- income support.

In addition, there is a scheme called Home Responsibilities Protection (HRP) which you may be eligible for (see page 30).

How many qualifying years do I need to get the full pension?

Your 'working life' is 49 years if you are a man and 45 years if you are a woman. If you were born before 5 July 1932, your working life may be shorter than this – check with the DSS.

- If 90 per cent or more of your 'working life' years are qualifying years, you are entitled to the full pension.
- If less than 25 per cent of your 'working life' years are qualifying years, you may not get any basic state pension at all.
- If you have between 25 per cent and 90 per cent of your working life as qualifying years your state pension will be reduced.

If you retire early

In some cases, if you retire early you may find that your entitlement to the basic state pension is significantly reduced.

- You cannot claim the basic state pension until you reach the state retirement age.
- If you are the wife of a man who has retired early and want to claim the spouse's pension based on his National Insurance

contribution record, you will have to wait until he reaches 65 before claiming.

Check with the DSS whether you should pay Class 3 voluntary contributions in order to counteract this effect.

If you are in a company pension scheme, check if it pays a 'bridging' pension to cover the period between early retirement and your state retirement age.

If you retire late

Currently you can defer your state pension by up to five years, which has the effect of increasing the amount when you claim. This works out at 7.5 per cent extra pension for each complete year you wait.

There are a few pitfalls, however.

- If you have retired abroad you are not allowed to defer the pension.
- If your spouse is claiming a pension based on your National Insurance record, he or she must agree to the deferment as well.
- You can't backdate a deferment.
- If you defer the pension and then start to claim within the five years, you can't defer for a second time.

If you are working after state retirement age you need to get a 'certificate of age exemption' from the DSS to show your employer so that you don't have any more National Insurance contributions deducted from your wages. If you are self-employed and working after the state retirement age, you don't have to make any more National Insurance contributions.

In the future, the rules on deferment are likely to become more generous.

Home Responsibilities Protection (HRP)

If you are at home caring for young children or elderly or sick relatives, you may be eligible for HRP. HRP reduces the number of qualifying years you need to get the full pension.

You are eligible for HRP if:

- you spend more than 35 hours a week caring for someone who receives attendance allowance, which is a benefit for the infirm

- you receive child benefit
- you receive income support.

The eligibility rules are likely to change frequently in the future. If you think that you may be eligible, contact the DSS – in some cases you will have HRP credited to you automatically, while in other cases you will have to apply for it after each tax year in which you were eligible.

Married women, the widowed or divorced

Married women

If you are a married woman and cannot claim the pension based on your own National Insurance contribution record, you can claim based on your husband's record. The pension is worth up to 60 per cent of the single person's pension. It is not payable until both you and your husband have reached state retirement age. You can defer it in the same way as with the normal pension if you wish (see page 107).

If you are a married woman who is receiving a single person's pension worth less than the married woman's pension, you will get the full married woman's pension when your husband starts claiming his pension.

If you are not living with your husband, you can still claim this pension. You should check with the DSS whether he has started claiming.

Widows and widowers

If you were widowed before you were 60, you have some choices when you reach 60.

- You can claim a pension.
- You can keep on receiving widow's benefit, if you are already receiving it, until you are 65 and then claim the pension.

- You can defer the pension, give up widow's benefit, and benefit from an increased pension when you claim (see page 107).

You should contact the DSS for advice on the best course to take in your particular circumstances.

If you are a widower, your position is similar, with a few complicated exceptions. The pension is based on your age and your wife's age when she died. Contact the DSS for advice on the best way to claim.

If you are divorced

If your marriage has been annulled or ended in divorce and you have not remarried, you may be able to claim the pension based on your spouse's contribution record. Get advice from the DSS.

——— Claiming the pension ———

There are four categories of basic pension:

- Category A is for people who are claiming their pension based on their own National Insurance contributions.
- Category B applies to you if you are basing your claim on your spouse's contributions.
- Category C applies only to people who could claim pensions by July 1948, so there are very few people left in this category.
- Category D is non-contributory, and is paid to people over 80 in certain circumstances (see page 33).

A few months before you reach state pension age, the DSS should send you form BR1 – if you haven't had it within three months of retirement age, you should get in touch with the DSS. The form will come with a letter giving information about the benefits you will receive; you can then decide whether to claim now, or to postpone it until later (see page 107).

You should make sure that you do claim in good time. The DSS will not backdate any claims for more than 12 months, and, in the case of claims for dependants, not more than 6 months.

If the DSS makes a mistake, you can ask for your case to be reviewed, and, if that doesn't work, you can appeal. The first step, though, if you think there has been a mistake, is to ask your local DSS office for a full explanation of how your pension has been assessed. Once you have received this, write to the DSS explaining what you think has gone wrong as soon as possible – there is a time limit on arrears, even if the DSS is at fault!

After you start claiming

The paperwork doesn't end with retirement, unfortunately! Here are some points to remember.

- Keep records of your pension receipts for your tax return.
- Tell the DSS about any changes to your legal status – for example, if your spouse dies, or you get divorced.
- If the DSS overpay you, they will want the money back.
- If you go into hospital for a long time, or into a residential home, your pension may be reduced.

If you are over 80

If you are 80 or older and are receiving state pension which is less than the Category D rate, your pension will be increased to this rate.

———————— Conclusion ————————

If you are under 40, the chances are that you will live to see the death of the basic state pension system as we know it today. Nevertheless, since most people are obliged to pay National Insurance contributions, or receive contribution credits, you should claim your entitlements when you are due for them. Pension advisers usually take the basic state pension into account when advising on pension planning – since it is currently around £3,000 a year, it is not to be sniffed at as a supplement to other pensions and savings.

Each year the government increases the basic state pension. The government can choose how much to increase it by, but usually it is kept in line with increases in the Retail Prices Index, which is a measure of inflation. Thus, the pension should keep up with inflation. Remember, though, that you will not have a worry-free old age if you are expecting to live on the basic pension by itself; take steps now to save for retirement in other ways.

4

PENSIONS FOR EMPLOYEES

There is no doubt that a really good employee scheme is the best pension scheme you can get, so long as you stay in it for long enough to build up full entitlements.

State Earnings Related Pension Scheme (SERPS)

If you have been an employee (but not if you have been self-employed), you may be entitled to benefits from SERPS. SERPS is a 'top up' state pension scheme into which employees who are liable to Class 1 National Insurance make contributions to enable them to receive taxable benefits from the state pension age.

Unlike the basic state pension, your entitlement to SERPS starts from the first time you contribute to it. If you are an employee who is not contracted out (see page 65) through an appropriate personal pension plan or a company scheme, you will be a member of SERPS automatically.

How much is the SERPS pension?

In the 1995/96 tax year, the maximum weekly SERPS pension you could receive was £94.12. Many people will receive much less than this, though, either because they weren't in SERPS for the whole period since it started in 1978, or because their earnings were low.

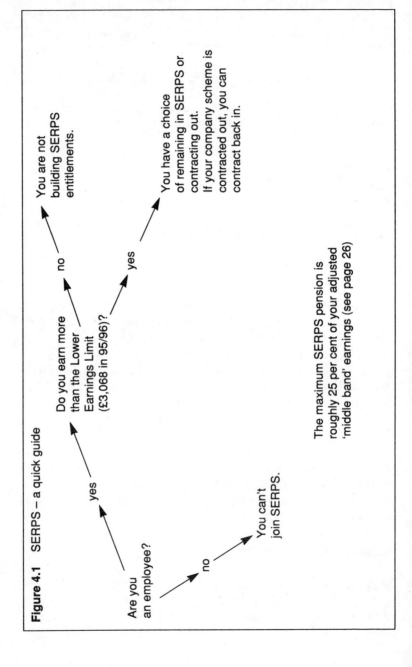

Figure 4.1 SERPS – a quick guide

Are you an employee?

yes

no → You can't join SERPS.

Do you earn more than the Lower Earnings Limit (£3,068 in 95/96)?

no → You are not building SERPS entitlements.

yes → You have a choice of remaining in SERPS or contracting out. If your company scheme is contracted out, you can contract back in.

The maximum SERPS pension is roughly 25 per cent of your adjusted 'middle band' earnings (see page 26)

The Government has reduced the amount of SERPS pension for people who are retiring after the 6 April 1999. This change, combined with the forthcoming changes to retirement ages for women (see page 21) and the chances of further changes in the future make the future value of a SERPS pension less for younger people than it is for people who have already retired or are just about to do so. In addition, the changes make it extremely complicated to work out what the future value of your SERPS pension will actually be, so, as with the basic state pension, it is best to rely on the DSS' pensions forecasting service (see page 22).

'Zero' earnings

In some cases you can be in SERPS but have your earnings disallowed in SERPS calculations. These are:

● if you are a married woman and pay your National Insurance contributions at the married woman's reduced rate;
● if you are making Class 3 voluntary National Insurance contributions;
● if you are receiving credits for National Insurance because you are receiving state benefits.

How your SERPS pension is worked out

As we saw in Chapter 3, page 26, you pay Class 1 National Insurance contributions if you earn more than a 'lower earnings level' (LEL), which in 1995/96 is £59 per week or £3,068 per year. If you earn more than the 'upper earnings level' (over £440 a week or £22,880 a year in 1995/96) you do not pay National Insurance on the amount you earn over the upper earnings level for that year.

The difference between the lower earnings level and the upper earnings level is called your 'middle-band' earnings. SERPS pensions cannot be more than roughly 25 per cent of your 'middle-band' earnings. This limit reduces to 20 per cent for employees retiring after the year 2000.

If you are retiring before the year 2000, the SERPS pension will be 1.25 per cent of middle-band earnings for each 20-year period after 1978, when SERPS was introduced. Because you have made contribu-

— **37** —

tions based on these earnings for many years, the State gives you, through SERPS, an additional pension based on these earnings. This can be quite a significant addition to your pension if you have been a high earner.

Working out your SERPS pension is complicated, and the DSS does it for you; however, for those who have a head for figures, here are the principles of how it is calculated.

1 Take your earnings up to the upper earnings level for each tax year for which you have paid Class 1 contributions in full between 1978 and the year you retire.
2 These earnings are then 'revalued'. This is done by multiplying each year's earnings by a figure which brings them in line with national average earnings for that year – you can obtain tables giving you these figures from the DSS.
3 Take away the lower earnings limit for the last complete tax year before you retired, from your revalued earnings for each year. The difference is called your 'surplus earnings'.
4 If you retire before the 6 April 1999, work out $\frac{1}{80}$ of each year's surplus earnings and add them together – this is the adjusted equivalent to 25 per cent of your average middle-band earnings, and gives you the figure for your SERPS pension.
5 If you are retiring after the 6 April 1999, the fraction of surplus earnings is reduced until, if you retire after the 6 April 2009, you will receive an adjusted equivalent of 20 per cent (down from 25 per cent) of your average middle-band earnings.

Contracting out of SERPS

If you have been a member of pension scheme that was 'contracted out' of SERPS then this pension scheme will have taken over responsibility for your SERPS entitlement and the government may not provide any additional pension at all.

Alternatively, you can 'contract out' of SERPS yourself into your own personal pension. This means that you will now pay lower rates of National Insurance, and all your pension contributions will be directed to your pension provider, who will have to provide all of your pension over and above the basic state old age pension. For a discussion of the pros and cons of contracting out, see Chapter 7.

SERPS is a very complex issue; you shouldn't make any moves concerning your pensions without considering SERPS in depth, with the help of a professional adviser. It is a good test of how good your pension advisers are to see whether or not they understand SERPS fully.

Help from the DSS

As with the basic pension, the DSS will give you a pensions forecast for SERPS. To apply for a forecast, get form BR19 from your local DSS office and send it to the Retirement Pensions Forecast and Advisory service (RPFA), whose address is on the form. After a few weeks they will send you details of:

- how much basic pension you have built up so far
- how much pension you will get if your employment circumstances don't change until you retire
- things you can do to increase the amount of pension you will get if you are not eligible for the full amount.

—————— Graduated pensions ——————

The graduated retirement benefit applies to you if you were employed between April 1961 and April 1975, and paid graduated National Insurance contributions. The pension is very low – in 1995/96 the weekly maximum is £6.57 for a man and £5.50 for a woman.

The amount you get is worked out from:

- the number of 'units' of graduated contributions you paid between April 1961 and April 1975
- the rate for a unit when you claim your pension.

To work out the pension,

1 Add up all your graduated contributions. If you don't already have this information, you can obtain it from the DSS.
2 If you are a woman, divide the total by 9. If you are a man, divide the total by 7.5
3 This gives you your units. The maximum number of units a man

can have is 86, and the maximum number of units a woman can have is 72.

4 Get leaflet NI 196, *Social Security Benefit Rates, Earnings Rules and NI Contribution Rates* from the DSS – this gives you the value of a unit (which are now increased in line with inflation).

5 Multiply the number of units by the value of a unit – this gives you the pension payable.

Equivalent Pension Benefit (EPB)

It is possible that you may have been contracted out of the graduated pension scheme by your employer. If so, the employer must pay you an equivalent to the graduated pension when you retire – this is called the Equivalent Pension Benefit (EPB).

Occupational pensions (for employees)

About half of all people who are employees in the United Kingdom are members of occupational pension schemes, and the total value of the funds is said to be around £500 billion. If you are a member of such a scheme, it is probably the most valuable benefit you get from working for your employer – after your salary, of course!

Occupational schemes can be generous. They are also 'tax efficient'; the contributions you make to the scheme are free of income tax, and your employer's contributions to your pension are tax deductible. The pension fund grows without being taxed, and, at present, you are allowed to take part of the pension as a lump sum when you retire. The only time you are taxed is when you receive your pension, which is taxed as if it were normal income.

Since a good occupational pension is so valuable, it is important to get to know as much about your scheme as possible so that you can make the most of it.

Not all employers provide pension schemes and, among those that do, the level of pension benefits they offer varies considerably. Occupational pension schemes can contract out all of their members from SERPS, and you can, as a private individual, decide to contract out through an appropriate personal pension plan (see page 65). Thus, most employees retiring in the United Kingdom will have two pensions:

- the basic state pension and SERPS

or

- the basic state pension and an occupational pension

or

- the basic state pension and a personal pension.

With one exception (see page 65) you can't, if you are a member of an occupational scheme, take out a personal pension as well, and, conversely, if you have a personal pension and then wish to join an employer's occupational scheme, you must stop contributing to your personal pension. In general, such changes don't mean that you actually lose what you have already paid into a scheme.

Collecting pensions

Increasingly, people are changing their employment status several times during their careers. At one time you might be an employee in an occupational scheme, at another you might be employed by a company which has no pension provision, and at other times you might be self-employed and ineligible for occupational pension schemes. This means that many people end up with a collection of small pensions, which may include:

- occupational pensions preserved in the schemes of previous employers
- pensions that have been transferred into pension products that are specifically designed to hold the 'transfer' (e.g. capital) value
- several different personal plans
- self-employed retirement annuities.

Leaving your company scheme

Company schemes are not compulsory. This means that you can opt out and go for a personal pension. There are some instances when you should do this. For example, if you think you will have a short time with the employer, say two or three years, then you may be better off

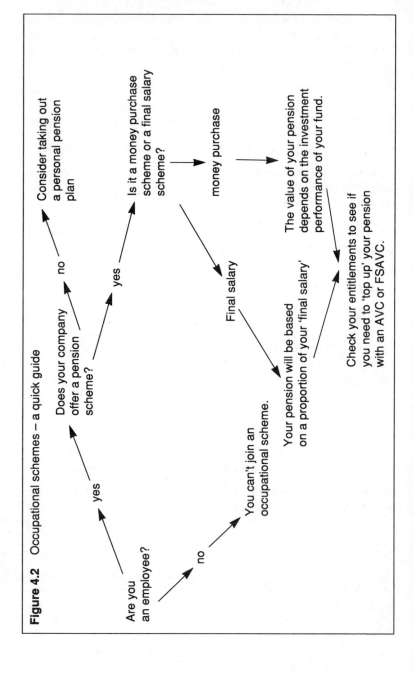

Figure 4.2 Occupational schemes – a quick guide

in a personal pension scheme that you intend to continue funding for a long time. Generally, though, company schemes are a better deal. The employer's contribution is valuable to you, especially if you are to stay in the scheme in the medium or long term.

Additionally, some schemes have guarantees. They say that when you retire you will get $\frac{1}{60}$ of your salary on retirement for every year that you worked. So if you worked for 30 years you will get $\frac{30}{60}$ of your final salary, or $\frac{1}{2}$. If you go out to a personal pension provider and try to copy those benefits, you will find it very expensive indeed.

Your employer's scheme may also be index linked or have increases during the payment of the pension. This, again, is extremely expensive to buy in your own right.

You must get a booklet detailing your employer's scheme rules and give it to your pension adviser. Ask him or her to put in writing a package of pension benefits which is as good as your employer's and work out the costs. You will then be comparing like with like and be able to make a sensible decision.

The variety of occupational schemes

Occupational schemes can be set up only by employers for the benefit of their own employees. The scheme can be small and include only a handful of senior employees or it can include all the employees of a large group of companies. There are also federated schemes available to employees of different firms in the same industry.

Your employer decides on the eligibility for membership of the scheme, chooses its benefits and defines its rules. Your employer may pay all the costs, in which case this scheme is called a 'non-contributory scheme'.

Employees may be required to contribute in which case it is called a 'contributory scheme' – normally you contribute a fixed percentage of salary deducted from your pay through your employer's payroll process; a typical contribution is 5 per cent or 6 per cent of salary.

Occupational pension schemes provide you with considerable tax benefits. In order to qualify for these, the scheme must conform to the rules of the Pension Schemes Office (PSO) and receive its formal approval. The PSO is the department of the Inland Revenue responsible for supervising and overseeing company pension schemes.

Public sector schemes

These include the pension schemes of nationalised industries and the statutory superannuation schemes for civil servants and other public servants such as National Health Service employees, lecturers and teachers, police officers and fire officers. Statutory superannuation schemes are unfunded and provide benefits on a pay-as-you-go basis; the pension funds of the nationalised industries hold enormous assets and are financially very powerful.

Private sector schemes

These are provided by private sector employers ranging from large public companies such as Shell or ICI to small firms, sole proprietors and partnerships (although, in all cases, only the employees can be members of a scheme). The Government Pension Schemes Office requires that private schemes not only fund their benefits but also that they can demonstrate that the fund's assets are enough to pay the benefits due to their members both now and in the future.

Funded schemes may be self-administered or insured schemes. Self-administered schemes manage their own investment of the contributions to provide the future pensions. They either employ their own investment specialists or they use outside professionals such as stockbroking firms to manage the fund for them. Insured schemes are run by insurance companies.

—— Final salary schemes ——

Also known as 'final pay schemes', these are the most common type, and link your pension to the amount of salary you are receiving just before you retire. They also depend upon the number of years you have been in the scheme.

Until 1988, companies had the right to compel their employees to join the company pension scheme, but with the introduction of personal pensions this is no longer so. Some companies make you a member of their scheme automatically when you start working for them, and it is up to you to tell the company that you want to opt out. The main reason for this is to give younger people, who may not be interested in pensions, the chance to start saving early in life.

How final salary pensions accumulate

The maximum pension the Inland Revenue allows you to take is ⅔, or $^{40}/_{60}$, of your final salary. This limit is lower for some high earners.

Most schemes work out your pension by giving you $^{1}/_{60}$ of your final salary for each year that you have been in the scheme. Thus, if you have been in the scheme for 40 years, you will have $^{40}/_{60}$ of your final salary as your pension.

Some schemes give $^{1}/_{80}$ of your final salary for each year of membership. This works out to $^{40}/_{80}$, or ½, of final salary if you stay in the scheme for 40 years.

There are a few very generous schemes – usually for top executives only – which give $^{1}/_{30}$ of your final salary for each year of membership. This means that you have to be a member of the scheme for only 20 years to get the maximum pension.

A point to note is that the definition of 'final salary' varies – it may be your pay at a particular date, the average annual pay over your last three years before retirement or some other formula.

The tax-free lump sum

The most you can take as a tax-free lump sum when you retire is 1.5 times your final salary after 40 years of membership.

How much can you contribute?

You can contribute up to a maximum of 15 per cent of your gross salary each year. Normally people contribute about 6 per cent. Your pension is calculated on your 'pensionable pay', and this is defined differently in different schemes. This can cause problems if, for example, you earn a lot of overtime but your scheme doesn't include this in 'pensionable pay'. In such cases, you can top up your pension through 'Additional Voluntary Contributions' (AVCs) – see page 46.

Some high earners have their pensions capped. For example, in 1995/96, members of final salary schemes who joined after June 1989 were limited to a 'pensionable salary' of £78,600. This caps their contributions, final salary and tax-free lump sum.

When can you retire?

It depends on your scheme. European Community Directives are forcing pension schemes to move towards equal retirement ages for men and women. In practice, schemes are tending to increase the retirement age for women from 60 to the male retirement age of 65, phased in over a long period. Some schemes operate a flexible period for retirement, but with a minimum age at which you can retire on full pension.

Additional Voluntary Contributions (AVCs)

These are for employees whose occupational pensions are not enough. You can make extra contributions to your pension, up to the tax limits, through an AVC scheme, which all employers' schemes must offer. AVCs either work as a 'money purchase' scheme, which means that your contributions are invested to build up a fund of cash, or to 'buy' extra years in schemes which are based on your years of membership. Most AVCs today are money purchase schemes.

About 90 per cent of people in occupational schemes do not contribute the maximum they are allowed to their main scheme. You will normally need to top up your pension if you have not worked for the same employer for 40 years. This can occur if:

- you have spent part of your working life being unemployed
- you have spent part of your working life being a student
- you have left work to raise a family
- you have changed jobs
- your scheme does not take all your earnings into account when calculating your pension
- you take early retirement
- you are self-employed for part of your life.

You can see why only 1 in 10 people build up full entitlements in occupational schemes!

AVCs give you:

- tax relief on your contributions
- tax-free growth on the pension fund
- a tax-free cash lump sum when you retire (this depends on how long you have been in the AVC).

The drawback with AVCs is that your employer does not contribute to the scheme, so there will be less money for your pension fund. Although your company sets up the AVC, it is usually subcontracted to an insurance company. You should get independent advice on whether it is worthwhile joining your company's AVC, since AVCs are not all alike, and a poor scheme can produce 20 per cent less growth in your pension fund than a good one.

Instead of using an AVC you can contribute to a 'Free Standing Additional Voluntary Contributions' scheme (FSAVC), which is separate from your employer's scheme.

Free Standing Additional Voluntary Contributions (FSAVCs)

These are for members of occupational schemes who want to top up their pension. They are an addition or an alternative to using AVCs and give you some privacy from your employer. Most of them are linked to unit trusts, and so they have an element of risk. Whether or not they are worthwhile depends entirely on your personal circumstances, so get professional advice. The main advantage that FSAVCs have over AVCs is that they give you a wide choice of providers and investments.

Questions to ask before joining an AVC or FSAVC

With the help of your adviser, you should establish the answers to the following:

- If I stay in my main scheme, will I build up two-thirds of my final salary as a pension?
- Has transferring to a new scheme in the past affected the value of my pension?
- Is my main scheme integrated into the state scheme?
- Have breaks in my employment record affected my pension?
- Do my overtime earnings and bonuses count towards my pension?
- Do I want to 'lock up' my top-up pension until I retire, or should I consider PEPs and TESSAs?
- Are any of the AVC or FSAVC charges paid by my employer?
- Is the AVC investment appropriate for my age?

- Do the trustees of the main scheme watch the performance of the AVC closely enough?
- Is the FSAVC good value?
- What are the penalties if I have to stop contributing to the scheme?

How much should you put into a pension scheme?

Having first decided how important pension income is in your total retirement plan, you need to decide on the actual cash amount you will contribute, based on your target income in retirement.

A final salary scheme guarantees you a certain fraction of your salary when you retire. Decide how much retirement income you will need, and ask your employer for a quotation of your likely benefits. If there is a gap between what you would actually need and what you are likely to get, then you will need funds for the difference, and you should ask your employer what schemes are available. Large group schemes often have low charges that make them efficient, and special arrangements for making up for any shortfall in your requirements.

You will need to decide whether you simply make additional voluntary contributions (AVCs) into a cash fund which will be converted into a pension when you retire, or whether you actually buy extra years in the scheme. You will undoubtedly need advice to make an important decision like this, and your Personnel Manager or the trustees of the scheme should be able to point you in the right direction. If you are seriously considering committing a reasonable proportion of your income to pension funding on this basis, it will be well worth paying £300 or so to a firm of consulting actuaries or to one of the top independent financial advisers to get to the truth.

Transferring the pension

Transferring the pension if you change jobs is complex, and is covered in detail in Chapter 7. You have several options, including leaving the pension where it is, or transferring the pension to your new employer's scheme.

Other benefits

These include:

- Death in Service benefits
- Death in Retirement benefits
- Discretionary benefits.

Death in Service benefits

Most company schemes provide you with a lump-sum death benefit. Ask for a 'form of nomination' so that you can put on that form the people whom you would like to benefit if you die. This gives the trustees of the scheme an idea of where you would like the money to go. If you die before your spouse then you may wish to leave everything to him or her, but consider what might happen if all your family were killed in a freak accident – who would you like to have the money then?

Death in Service benefits may include a pension of up to ⅔ of your earnings at death for a dependent adult, plus pensions for dependent children.

Check to see if your scheme limits payment of these benefits to spouses only and if there are special rules for pension payments to partners who were not married to you.

Death in Retirement benefits

These are similar to Death in Service benefits – good schemes will give around ⅔ of the member's pension to a spouse plus a pension for any dependent children.

Discretionary benefits

These are benefits which the scheme may or may not give to you – the decision is in the hands of the trustees. Such benefits include pension increases over the annual guaranteed level.

Final salary schemes – checklist

Here is a checklist to help you assess your employer's scheme:

- When is the pension payable?
- What is the rate at which the pension builds up? (Is it at ⅟₆₀ of final pay for each year you work, or at some other rate?)
- What is the scheme's definition of 'pensionable earnings'? (Are all your earnings included?)
- How is the 'final salary' calculated? (Is it your earnings in the year before you retire, or worked out on some other formula?)
- How does the scheme define 'pensionable service'? (For example, does it count maternity leave?)
- How much can I take as a tax-free lump sum when I retire?
- How is the pension increased after retirement? (Preferably it should be inflation proofed, for example by linking it to the Retail Prices Index).
- What if I retire early because of ill health? (A good scheme will give you a pension as if you had remained in the job until normal retirement, but based on your salary level when you left).
- What are the Death in Service and Death in Retirement benefits?
- What if I leave the scheme? (If you opt for a preserved pension, it should be linked to the Retail Prices Index.

—— Money purchase schemes ——

Money purchase schemes are designed differently from final salary schemes.

- The amount of your pension depends upon the performance of the pension fund as well as on other factors.
- Death benefits tend to be lower.
- Most schemes have a separate fund for each member, which is used to buy an annuity when you retire, as with personal pensions.
- Most schemes do not give disability and medical insurance.

While money purchase schemes can be just as good as final salary schemes, many of them are not. It is important to examine your scheme carefully to check if it is good value, and whether you will need to top it up. To understand the principles on which all money purchase schemes are run, you should read Chapter 5, 'Personal Pensions', where they are explained in detail.

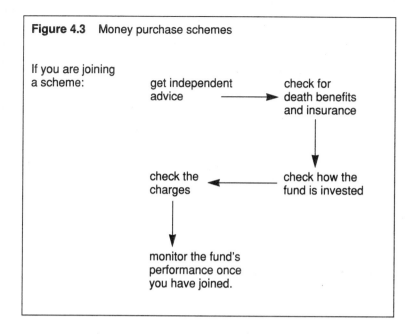

Figure 4.3 Money purchase schemes

Three kinds of money purchase scheme

The three main kinds of money purchase scheme are:

1 *Contracted-in money purchase schemes (CIMPS)*
   These are contracted in to SERPS, and the pension is on top of the SERPS pension. You can join a CIMP and contract out of SERPS using an 'appropriate personal pension' (see Chapter 7).
2 *Contracted-out money purchase schemes (COMPS)*
   These are contracted out of SERPS, and thus your National Insurance contributions are lower. Most COMPS give you a 'protected rights' pension which is a substitute for SERPs benefits, as with the GMP (see page 93), but the value is not guaranteed.
3 *Group personal pensions (GPPs)*
   GPPs are similar to personal pensions (see Chapter 5). You may contract out of SERPS if you wish. In general, a COMP will give you better value than a GPP, but it depends on your circumstances, so you should seek advice.

Your contributions

Although a good money purchase scheme can be just as valuable as a final salary scheme, in some cases employers have set them up as a cheap way of fulfilling their obligations, so you need to make sure that your scheme will give you an adequate pension. As a rule of thumb, if you are under 35, the total annual contributions by you and your employer should be about 7 per cent to match an average final salary scheme. This percentage should rise to 15 per cent by the time you are 55.

Some employers match your contributions by the same amount; this is valuable, since the more you put in, the more the employer will, too.

Money purchase schemes – checklist

As always, you will need an adviser to help you decide whether or not to join a scheme. The main points to check are:

- What are the death and disability benefits? These tend to be lower than in final salary schemes, so you may need to buy extra insurance separately.
- Who is providing the scheme? If you are not happy with the provider, you should consider another way of saving for retirement.
- How is the money invested? In general, when you are young, most of your pension money should be invested in the stock market, and when you are nearing retirement, most of it should be in fixed-interest investments.
- What are the charges for in the scheme? This is a very important question, as we will see in Chapter 5, because the higher the charges are, the less your money will grow.
- Are there penalties if you leave or move the scheme?

Divorce

At present, if you get divorced in Scotland, pension entitlements are usually divided equally between the spouses when the divorce settlement is calculated. In England and Wales, however, the division of the pension is up to the courts, so sometimes one spouse loses out. The law is likely to change in the near future to make this fairer.

——————— Maternity leave ———————

If you take paid maternity leave your pension rights are protected by law, although you still have to continue making the contributions. Women sometimes get a raw deal in occupational schemes, so you should check the rules carefully and keep up to date on them. EU legislation will bring in many changes over the next few years in an attempt to make pension schemes fairer for women.

—— How safe are private sector occupational schemes? ——

Most occupational schemes are probably perfectly safe. Public sector schemes are the safest, since they are backed by the government. However, the scandal of Robert Maxwell's misuse of his employees' pension funds shows that they are not always safe. Broadly speaking, there are many good safeguards against the misappropriation of funds, but a really determined crook who controls a company may be able to find ways around them.

Robert Maxwell took hundreds of millions of pounds' worth of pension fund assets from the occupational schemes in Maxwell Communications Corporation and Mirror Group Newspapers, both of which were large companies quoted on the stock market. He used this money to fend off his bankers when he got into financial difficulties by borrowing too much for his many business ventures. This was entirely illegal, but he was able to do it by outsmarting the regulators and the trustees of the funds. When his empire crashed, many employees faced drastically reduced pensions, and the government stepped in with a loan to the pension funds to help pay out the pensions. It is still unclear whether everyone in the scheme will be assured of receiving their full pensions.

How can you protect against this danger? One thing you can do is to try to become a trustee of the pension fund, or, if you are unable to do that, make sure that you monitor the accounts and reports of your scheme closely. Trusts are discussed in the next section.

An insured pension fund will be safer than many company-run arrangements. For example, the Policyholders Protection Act means

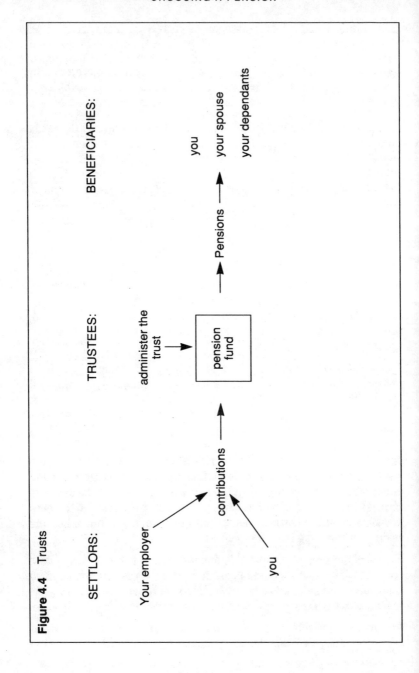

Figure 4.4 Trusts

SETTLORS:

Your employer

you

contributions

TRUSTEES:

administer the trust

pension fund

BENEFICIARIES:

Pensions

you
your spouse
your dependants

that members of an insured scheme would be far more likely to get their pension benefits paid by seeking them from the insurer than they would if the company went into liquidation. If the employer never paid the insurance company then he or she could still run off with your money, so always get regular statements of your policy values.

It is a frightening thought that your occupational pension may not be safe from executive thieves. Remember that your pension is your money, so look after it! Make sure that you monitor all the arrangements on an ongoing basis, and use an independent professional to back you up. If you think something is wrong, don't just hope that it will work out by itself – take action, both by writing to the regulatory authorities and by looking at the possibility of leaving the scheme.

Trusts

Most occupational schemes have their pension funds held in trust, which is a special way of holding assets in law.

The idea of the trust is an extraordinarily subtle and legal concept invented by English lawyers centuries ago. A trust is not a person in law in the way that a company or an individual is. Thus it can't 'own' anything itself – the assets of the trust are 'vested' in the trustees, who can be companies or individuals.

One way of thinking of a trust is to say that it is a kind of slow-motion gift from the 'settlor', who puts the money in, to the 'beneficiaries', who take the money out.

As a member of an occupational scheme you are both a settlor, because you are paying in your contributions, and a beneficiary, because the trust is going to pay you your pension. This gives you many legal rights to know how the funds in the trust are being handled.

The trustees are the people who look after the money in the meantime. They are usually paid to do this. The money in the trust can be in any form under UK law, so it could be a mixture of cash, property, investments and insurance policies. The money is under the control of the trustees who act as caretakers with specific duties and responsibilities.

The trust instrument

A trust can be created by various documents; it is not in itself a holding company, a contract or a will, but it can be created by these, as well as by a gift from the settlor during his or her lifetime. The document creating the trust may be called:

- the trust deed
- the trust agreement
- the trust instrument
- the settlement
- the declaration of trust.

Normally it is called a trust deed. This document sets out the rules of the trust, including:

- the powers of the trustees
- how the trustees can resign
- the benefits of the pension scheme
- the pension age
- the rules on early and late retirement
- what happens if you leave the scheme
- the rules on the tax-free cash lump sum.

If you want to know how your scheme is run, you must get hold of a copy of the trust deed.

The history of trusts

In the Middle Ages when life was cheap, people were often in danger of losing what they had to an aggressor.

During the Crusades, a problem arose for land-owning knights who were setting off for the East, perhaps never to return. While the knight was away, there was the real danger that someone would try to grab all or part of his land, and his wife and children would not be able to take legal action to prevent this. This was because litigation could be started only by an adult male who had good grounds for claiming that he had a better title to the land than the person who was trying to steal it.

Thus the trust was born; in its first incarnation, it simply meant that the crusading knight would give his land to a trusted male friend to hold 'for the use of' the knight's family while he was away, the understanding being that the friend would take legal action to protect the estate, if necessary. If the friend turned out to be a crook and refused to give the land back when the knight returned, the only thing the knight could do was petition the king directly for the return of the property.

By the middle of the sixteenth century this unsatisfactory state of affairs had been improved upon, and holding an estate 'for the use of' someone else came to be called a trust. The legal owner, or trustee, was compelled by law to use the assets he was holding on trust for the benefit of the beneficiaries, and not for himself or anyone else. This is the principle underlying modern trusts; trustees are not allowed to use the trust's assets for their own benefit, but only for the beneficiaries.

Becoming a trustee

If you have the opportunity to become a trustee, you will need to get some training. Contact the National Association of Pension Funds for information – the address is on page 157.

In 1997, a new Pensions Act will come into force which will require schemes to have a minimum number of trustees on the board who are actually members of the scheme. The minimum will probably be a third. Since the duties and responsibilities of a trustee are heavy, not everyone will want to become a trustee. If you think you can do the job, you should put yourself forward – you may find that it is very interesting and rewarding work, and you will know exactly what is going on in your scheme.

The legal responsibilities of a trustee are great. Among other things, they must:

- understand the standards of regulation;
- hold the trust funds for the benefit of the beneficiaries and can only do things with the trust fund which the trust deed says that they can;
- use the utmost diligence in carrying out their duties. This means,

for example, that they must avoid making financial losses with the trust fund;

- keep proper accounts;
- obey the laws relating to trusts and the obligations imposed by the trust deed;
- act in the best interests of the beneficiaries;
- not put themselves in a position where there is a possibility of a conflict between their personal self-interest and their duty to the trust. For instance, trustees cannot sell their own property to the trust or buy trust property for themselves.

Since trusts are not 'legal persons', it is the trustees who can sue or be sued. For this reason, you will need to have insurance in case something goes wrong.

As an ordinary member of a scheme, what information am I entitled to?

You are entitled to a lot of information about your pension, including how your pension scheme is being run. This includes:

- *Trust deeds and rules*
  You may inspect documents governing the trust once a year, and obtain copies for a 'reasonable' fee. So can your spouse and other beneficiaries, such as your children.
- *Statements of benefits and transfer values*
  You are entitled to one free statement a year.
- *A basic explanation of the rules and benefits*
  This must be sent to you within 13 weeks of joining the scheme.
- *The annual report*
  You are entitled to a copy of this on request.
- *The audited accounts*
  You may inspect these.
- *Actuarial reports and statements*
  These are done every three years or so; they are professional assessments of the value and adequacy of the funds. You may inspect them, or keep a copy if you pay a 'reasonable fee'.

—— If your company is wound up ——

Although the funds in company schemes are kept separate from the company's own money, if your company is wound up – in other words if it goes bust or is closed down – it can affect your scheme. Here's how:

- Your pension income could be delayed.
- You could find yourself with lower benefits.
- There will probably be a period when you have trouble finding out what is going on, and who is looking after the scheme.

When a company is wound up, an independent trustee is appointed to look after the scheme. You should find out who this is, and write to him or her to make sure that your personal details are correct. Remember to keep copies of all correspondence, and notes of any telephone conversations. Ask the new trustee for full information about:

- your employer's contributions
- the level of benefits
- annual increases to deferred pensions
- discretionary benefits.

If you think that the company is breaking the law, you should contact the Occupational Pensions Advisory Service (see page 158 for the address).

———— Working abroad ————

If your company sends you abroad, your pension arrangements will be affected. If you are away for only a year, you can probably continue with your existing plan, particularly if you are working in another EU country, even if you are compelled to participate in the host country's plan as well.

Some companies have international plans that are run from tax havens; these may offer:

- a minimum pension level based on the employee's length of service.
- help with calculating the accumulated pension rights from different countries around the world where the expatriate has worked.
- help with reconciling rights in different schemes from different companies which have been acquired or merged.

International plans tend to be in tax havens in order to maximise tax saving, avoid state regulation and ensure flexibility in investment. You may have some say in how these investments are handled, which is desirable. What you get out of such a scheme will vary enormously, but it will be in one of the following forms:

- a guaranteed pension for life which is based on what you were earning when you retired and how long you worked for the company.
- a lump sum paid on retirement or on leaving the company.
- an annuity.

If you are lucky enough to be sent to a low-tax country for several years, you will have a great opportunity to save a large part of your salary. For most of us, a spell as an expatriate is probably the best chance we have of rapidly accumulating capital; however, many expats fail to do this successfully during their time abroad.

The principal benefits are:

- Your salary is not subject to the overheads of living at home.
- In many cases you may receive your pay net of tax.
- You may be working in a country with a 0 tax regime, for example if you work in parts of the Middle East.
- Many expats enjoy free or subsidised housing overseas.
- You can receive an income by letting your house at home.
- Expat packages often include paid education for children, company cars, 100 per cent health cover and big expense allowances.
- You may receive a 'foreign service premium' and a cost of living allowance which you do not need to spend.
- In countries with a low cost of living, the adaptable expat can reduce living expenses massively by living and eating as the locals do.

Example

Suppose you are on a 3-year assignment and find you can save £6,000 a month – which is not an impossible figure for many professionals. By the end of your term you should be able to accumulate around £250,000 in safe investments, without having paid tax on the interest or any capital gains tax. By getting your contract of employment right and investing wisely, you can accumulate a substantial sum for your retirement.

Conclusion

If you have a demanding career with a large company it is vital to fully understand your employer's arrangements for your pension, salary and other allowances before you agree to a spell abroad. Pay a specialist adviser a fee to 'hold your hand' while you negotiate with your employer.

5

PERSONAL PENSIONS

Very many people, both employees and the self-employed, are unable to join a company pension scheme. If you are in this position you should consider taking out a personal pension plan.

Personal pensions were introduced in 1988; it was thought that a pension that you could carry with you when moving in and out of different employment situations was an important extension of choice for individuals. The plans replaced a scheme for self-employed retirement annuities and, for the first time, allowed individual employees to contract out of SERPS, receiving a repayment of some National Insurance contributions to help start a personal plan.

As we saw in Chapter 4, the Government will reduce the value of SERPS over the next 20 years, so it is unlikely that SERPS or a personal plan funded solely by the National Insurance contribution rebate, will give you a decent pension when you retire.

Thus, taking out a personal pension plan is essential for many people. Personal pension plans have had some bad publicity in recent years; during the 1980s many people were badly advised by salespeople, and joined inappropriate schemes. Although this particular form of malpractice has been cleared up, it is very important to understand these schemes properly and get professional advice before committing yourself – otherwise, high charges and poor investment performance could lead to a low pension.

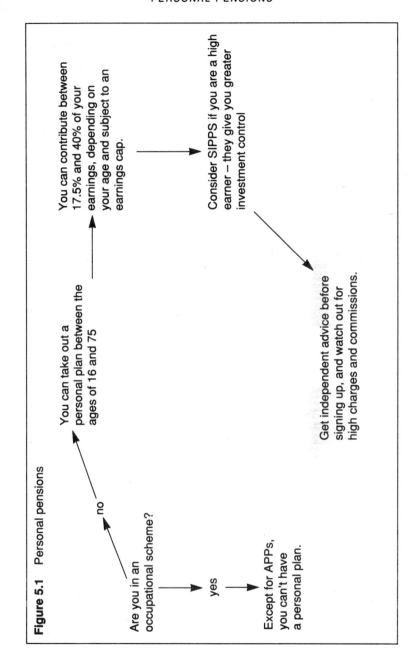

Figure 5.1 Personal pensions

Are you in an occupational scheme?

yes

Except for APPs, you can't have a personal plan.

no

You can take out a personal plan between the ages of 16 and 75

You can contribute between 17.5% and 40% of your earnings, depending on your age and subject to an earnings cap.

Consider SIPPS if you are a high earner – they give you greater investment control

Get independent advice before signing up, and watch out for high charges and commissions.

Who provides personal pensions?

They are provided by financial institutions, such as:

- banks
- building societies
- unit trust groups
- insurance companies
- friendly societies.

These organisations are well regulated, and invest the vast pension funds they control diversely in order to make them grow. Much of the money is invested in industry by means of the stock market.

The main features of personal plans

For employees, there are two parts to the plans: the 'appropriate' personal plan, which is used to contract out of SERPS, and a top-up pension, which is used for extra contributions. Normally providers lump the two together to make plans less confusing.

N.B. If you are self-employed, the 'appropriate' plans do not apply to you.

As with other pension schemes, personal plans give you:

- tax-free growth of the pension fund
- full tax relief on your contributions
- up to 25 per cent of the top-up part of the fund can be taken as a lump sum tax free when you retire.

What personal plans cannot give you is the contributions made by an employer, so if you are an employee with access to a generous company scheme, you will probably be better off staying with that scheme. If you are already in a company scheme, think carefully before transferring out into a personal plan – in most cases you will lose out by doing so (see page 95).

Personal plans are all 'money purchase schemes' (see Chapter 4), so they are not linked to your final salary. Your contributions are invested for you, and the value of the annuity you buy when you retire will vary, depending on, among other things, how much the provider has charged you and how well the fund has performed.

Who can take out a personal pension plan?

Anyone who is aged between 16 and 75 can take out a personal pension, but you can't have a personal plan *and* be in an employer scheme unless:

- your employer scheme gives only death benefits
- you have earnings outside what you receive from your main employer – for instance, if you occasionally work as a freelance
- you are using the personal plan only to contract out of SERPS
- you are taxed on your employer's contributions to your employer scheme

— 'Appropriate' personal pensions —

These are designed for:

- employees who cannot join an occupational scheme
- employees whose occupational scheme is contracted in to SERPS.

If you are a woman under 35 or a man under 40 and you earn more than £8,500 a year, opting out of SERPS and taking out an appropriate pension plan could be beneficial. This is because there is a rebate of National Insurance contributions which will often outweigh the value of the SERPS benefits you are giving up.

The rebate

The DSS sends the rebate to your pension provider after the tax year ends. It is calculated as a percentage of your middle-band earnings; the maximum rebate in 1996/97 if you are under 30 is 1.8% of your National Insurance contribution, plus 3% of your employer's contribution, plus 0.57% tax relief, totalling 5.37%. If you are aged 30 or over, there is an additional incentive of 1%.

Protected rights

The rebate money is called your 'protected rights'. It doesn't count towards the tax-free lump sum you can take on retirement, and usually you must take the pension at the state retirement age. One advantage, though, is that when you buy the annuity on retirement it must give a spouse's pension worth 50 per cent of your pension and the annuity payment has to increase by 3 per cent each year.

Top-up pensions

Since the 'appropriate pension' will not be enough on its own, you can take out a 'top-up' personal plan as well. The legal limit on how much you can contribute to a top-up plan in any one year is calculated as a percentage of 'net relevant earnings' (NREs). If you miss contributing in a year, it is possible to 'carry back' a contribution a little later – ask your adviser about this. It is also possible to 'carry forward' unused tax relief from the last six years.

- If you are an employee, your NRE is your gross earnings less 'allowable business expenses', which, in practice, few people have, so your NRE will probably be your gross remuneration.
- Your employer can contribute to your top-up plan, but does not have to do so by law.
- If you are self-employed, your NRE is much more complicated to work out. Get your accountant to do it for you.

The following table shows how much of your NRE you can contribute to your pension in any one year, according to your age:

Age at 6 April	% of NREs
35 or under	17.5
36–45	20
46–50	25
51–55	30
56–60	35
61–74	40

Example for people under 36

Suppose you are 27 and are getting established in a career, and that your NREs are £25,000. The most you can contribute in a year to your personal pension is 17.5 per cent of £25,000 = £4,375.

Other features of top-up plans

You can run more than one top-up plan at the same time as long as your total contributions are under the limits for your age. The other main points are:

The earnings cap

If you have a high salary, you may not be able to make contributions up to the limit for your age. This is because of the 'earnings cap' which, for the 1995/96 tax year, is £78,600. Thus, for example, if you are aged between 46 and 50, you would be able to contribute only 25 per cent of £78,600 in 1995/96, even if you were earning more than this.

Life insurance

You can use up to 5 per cent of the contribution limit to pay life insurance premiums, giving you tax relief on the payments – often, however, the plan provider's life assurance rates are high and you can get better deals buying insurance elsewhere, in spite of losing the tax relief on the premiums.

— Group personal pension schemes —

These are sometimes used by small firms instead of setting up an occupational pension scheme. As an employee, you have your own personal pension policy, which is portable and transferable if you move jobs, and you can use it to decide whether or not to contract out of SERPS. You decide how much to contribute to the scheme (within the legal limits). The employer is free to contribute to your pension or not, and can contribute different amounts to different employees' schemes.

Before joining a group scheme, you should check the details carefully, in particular the penalties for making changes later:

- If you change jobs and are offered a good company scheme, you will have to give up your personal plan – so make sure the penalties are not too high.
- If you arrange to make no further contributions to your plan, it becomes 'paid up'; this may also attract penalties.
- Check to see how your life assurance is being paid; is it taken from your contributions, or your employer's?

If your group personal plan is run on a 'nil commission' basis, you will find it much easier to understand the cost structure, and there are no penalties. The adviser is paid a fee, and you can see what you are paying for at all times.

—— Retirement annuity contracts ——

These were no longer sold after the introduction of personal pensions in 1988, but if you had already taken out a retirement annuity contract, you are still allowed to contribute to it. The contribution limits are a little lower than the personal pension limits as a percentage of your salary, but there is no earnings cap (see page 67).

The contribution limits are:

Age at 6 April	% of NREs
50 or under	17.5
51–55	20
56–60	22.5
61–74	27.5

If you have a retirement annuity contract you may not contract out of SERPS. Here are some points to check:

- What are the benefits if you die before retiring? Some types of contract give poor returns in these cases.
- Was the agreement written under trust? If not, check with a tax adviser for possible effects on inheritance tax on your estate when you die.

It is possible to take out a personal plan as well as continuing to contribute to your retirement annuity contract, but you will need professional help to keep within the complicated rules governing this.

— Self-invested (self-administered) — personal plans (SIPPS/SAPPS)

SIPPS gives you more choice and control over how your pension fund is invested. If you are a relatively high earner, and have investment experience, this freedom of choice may be particularly appealing.

Personal plan providers often do not invest your pension funds them-selves – they pay a professional fund manager or stockbroker to do it

for them. SIPPS separate the charges for administration and investment, and give you the choice either to decide on the investments
yourself, or to pay a stockbroker of your choice to do it for you.

The charges for SIPPS can be high, so you must take care to get
independent advice before committing yourself. To make it worthwhile, you probably need a transfer value of at least £50,000, or annual
contributions of more than £20,000.

Pension mortgages

You can use a personal plan to raise a mortgage. It is similar to an
endowment mortgage in that you pay interest on the loan each
month, and when you take your pension you use the tax-free lump
sum to pay off the debt.

In general, this is not a good idea. Here are four reasons why:

1 Pension plans are for your retirement income. If you use the
   tax-free lump sum to pay off your mortgage, you will have less to
   live on when you retire.
2 This arrangement reduces the flexibility of the pension plan. You
   could lose money if you surrendered your plan for some reason, or
   if you had to stop paying into the plan because you joined an
   occupational pension scheme.
3 The Inland Revenue does not approve of pension mortgages, so the
   technicalities of the agreement become complicated – this could
   lead to loss.
4 Why do you want a pension mortgage? If it is because you can't
   afford both a pension and a mortgage, you may be trying to stretch
   your finances too far – thus increasing the risk of repossession.

Pension mortgages can sometimes be advantageous to wealthy people
with secure incomes. If you are in this category, you should seek
professional advice on the matter.

The danger of high charges

Most personal plans are offered by life insurance companies, but
other providers include friendly societies, unit trusts, building

societies and banks. As well as your freedom of choice over which provider to use, you can also select from a wide variety of plans.

Making the right choice is important. If you take out a plan that has high charges and turns out to give poor investment returns, your pension will suffer. Ideally, you should try to find a plan that has low charges and performs well.

One way of assessing a plan is to see how long it takes for your contributions to pay for the provider's charges and then catch up with inflation. Once you have achieved this, your fund starts making money for you; in the case of an expensive plan, this could be up to half the lifetime of the policy.

Example

Carol wants to pay £100 a month into a personal pension plan which is to last for 25 years. She and her advisers make an educated guess at the average annual growth of the fund and the inflation rate over the life of the plan – they think it will grow at 8 per cent a year, and that the average annual inflation rate will be 5 per cent a year.

- If she could find a plan which had no charges except for a 5 per cent charge when she invested, her fund would catch up with inflation and charges after 3 years and 5 months.
- If she found a similar plan which had an additional monthly administration charge of only £3, her fund would catch up with inflation and charges after 5 years and 9 months.
- If she found a similar plan which had a further charge of 75 per cent of her first year's premiums, which is lower than the sum many providers currently charge, it would take her 12 years before her fund had caught up with charges and inflation.

Avoiding high charges

Unless you are a whiz at financial maths and you know all the tricks that providers might get up to, you will need independent professional help to work out the real cost of a plan. Some will assess your plans for a fee of under £200 – this is worth doing, since high charges can ruin your hopes of a good pension. Remember, though, that no one can predict exactly how well investments will perform, so you won't know what your pension will be for certain until it is time to retire. As a rule of thumb, you can expect only 3 per cent or 4 per cent annual growth after inflation.

— Types of personal pension plan —

Unless you decide to opt for a SIPPS plan you will be relying on the provider to take the investment decisions regarding your fund. Investment is in itself a vast subject; the more you learn about investment the better, but until you have acquired a lot of experience as an investor, it is sensible to allow professionals to do it for you. Nevertheless, you will still need to choose from four different types of plan:

- unit-linked plans
- unit and investment-trusts
- with-profits plans
- unitised with-profits plans
- deposit-based plans.

Unit-linked plans

Insurance companies offer unit-linked plans. Your contributions to the plan buy 'units' in a pension fund which is a collection of many people's contributions. The value of a unit goes up and down according to the current market value of the invested fund. For this reason, it is important to know the level of risk that is being taken with the fund.

The plan literature will tell you what kind of risk will be taken with the fund – the range will be from low-risk deposits, UK government bonds (gilts) and index-linked funds, to medium risks such as funds which invest in established shares, right up to high-risk investments such as shares in companies in the 'emerging markets' of the developing world. As a general rules, the higher the risk, the higher the possible return, but you shouldn't use your pension fund for gambling, so a sensible choice would be for medium-risk investments such as 'managed funds', which spread their investments across various other investment funds operated by the pension provider.

Charges for unit-linked plans

These plans have a large number of charges:

- About a 5 per cent initial charge when you purchase units from most plans.
- Between 0.5 per cent and 1.5 per cent of the value of your units as an annual management charge.

- There may be surrender charges, in which case if you stop making contributions to the plan, or if you transfer it in the early years, you are likely to be credited with only part of the value of your plan.
- You may be charged if you switch your contributions from one fund to another, though the first switch, or two, each year may be free.
- Possibly a commission for the adviser who sells you the plan. This can be 70 per cent of the value of your first year's premiums, but may be taken out over a longer period.
- You may be allocated 'capital units' in the first years of the plan; these have a much higher management charge – for example, 3 per cent or 5 per cent of the value of the fund. You usually carry on paying this higher charge throughout the life of the plan.
- There may be a policy fee or an administration charge, which is deducted regularly to cover the costs of the paperwork involved in running the plan.
- There may be a low 'allocation' rate of your premiums in the early years of your plan; what is happening is that the provider is deducting a fairly high proportion (typically 30 per cent) from your premiums during an 'initial period'.
- Single premiums may be charged at around 5 per cent per contribution. Over the whole life of the plan, this should work out to be a cost equivalent to what you pay if you are making regular contributions.

If possible, arrange to pay a fee to your adviser in return for the removal of all the commission-type charges, or opt for the single-premium system, which gives you more flexibility.

Unit trust and investment trust plans

These offer similar schemes to unit-linked plans. Your premiums buy units in a pool of investments, and the value of the units varies with the value of the underlying investments. In the same way as with unit-linked plans, there are different types of investment trust and unit trust, and you can use a managed fund or mixed unit trust to get a spread of different investments.

Usually you may invest in more than one fund at once, but there may be a minimum amount of investment for each one. Check that you can switch between the different funds or trusts after you have started the plan.

Charges for unit trust and investment trust plans

Unit trusts and investment trusts are required by law to be clear about the charges they make. Charges can be high, though, and you may find that some investment trusts represent better value than unit trusts. Typical charges include:

- The 'bid-offer' spread. This is an initial charge of about 5 per cent. 'Bid-offer' refers to the difference between the price you buy your unit at (the 'offer' price) and the price you get if you sell them (the 'bid' price) – if you sold the units immediately, the bid price would be about 5 per cent lower than the offer price.
- An annual management charge of about 1 per cent.
- A single administration charge when you take out the plan, or during the first year.
- If the unit trust pays commissions to advisers, it will be on a single premium basis, giving you more flexibility than if you signed up for regular payments.
- Any charges for stopping your contributions or reducing the amounts.
- Switching unit trusts can be expensive if you sell units in one trust and buy units in another. Some unit trust plans use 'umbrella funds', which include several different funds, and you can switch between these either for free or at low cost.

With-profits plans

These plans are offered by insurance companies, who invest your money mainly in the United Kingdom and international shares, property and bonds. The agreements are extremely complex and can be confusing.

With-profits plans use a system of bonuses. With the 'traditional' with-profits plan, you are guaranteed a substantial bonus at the end of a predetermined investment period. There may be additional annual bonuses called 'reversionary' bonuses. Once they have been added, reversionary bonuses can't be taken away, so the amount in your plan can't fall. The level of future reversionary bonuses isn't guaranteed, however, and depends on the provider.

There is also usually a 'terminal' bonus which may be added at the end of the plan period, depending on how well the fund has performed in its final year.

The bonus system has the effect of making the return on personal plans more predictable than with unit-type plans, since the bulk of the bonuses are guaranteed.

Currently, the trend for with-profits plans is for the providers to increase the value of the 'terminal' bonus at the expense of the guaranteed bonuses – terminal bonuses may represent 60 per cent of the total value of your pension fund when you retire. This has the effect of making with-profits plans less predictable, since you cannot be sure what the terminal bonus will be when you start the plan.

Charges for with-profits plans

It is difficult to know exactly what you are paying in charges with with-profits plans. This is because the charges are taken out of the fund before the bonuses are declared. The only exception is a monthly policy fee, but this is only a small part of the charges you will pay.

Unitised with-profits plans

These are a newer version of with-profits plans and include some of the benefits of unit-linked plans. They are sold by insurance companies and can either be a separate plan, or an option within a unit-linked plan.

The bonus system used is different from those in with-profits plans – some providers simply increase the value of your units instead of giving a bonus, while others give extra units as a bonus. The majority of providers do give some guarantees over bonuses but about a quarter do not.

Deposit-based plans

These are simply pension funds which are invested in cash deposits, at banks, building societies or on the money markets. The fund grows as interest is added to it, just as normal cash savings do. Future interest rates are not guaranteed, and if your plan has many years to run, the chances are that the fund may not beat inflation.

Charges for deposit-based plans

The rate of interest you receive on the fund will be adjusted downwards so that the provider's expenses in managing the plan are covered. Sometimes there will be a separate administration fee or similar charge as well.

Which one of the five types of plan is best for me?

The investments which involve the most risk generally also have the best growth potential, but while you want your pension plan to perform well, you would not be wise to take big risks with the fund. After all, the most important aim of the fund is that it is still there when you retire!

Unit-linked plans, unit trusts and investment trusts are more risky than with-profits plans, because in the former schemes the value of your investments can fall as well as rise. You can lessen this risk to some degree by choosing less risky types of fund, where you are offered a choice. In one sense, deposit-based schemes can be said to be the least risky of the five types, since the amount of the fund can't fall, but because the funds are invested in cash, the effects of inflation tend to make this kind of plan give the lowest returns.

In the context of pensions, you shouldn't worry unduly about investment risk, though. Pension funds are simply not allowed to be invested in highly dubious ventures – they go mainly into well-established, well-funded investments, so you are, in effect, betting on the future stability of the UK economy; short of a very major crisis, the chances are good that your pension fund will still be there when you retire.

If you have many years to go before retirement, it makes sense to choose the slightly more risky plans – unit-linked and unit trust investments – since these offer a good chance of giving you a good return over the long term. You can mitigate the extra risk to some degree by choosing a managed fund or mixed trust rather than the more specialised funds.

If you are getting closer to retirement – say within ten years – then it may be worthwhile to invest part or all of your money in a with-profits plan.

When you're very close to retirement – within five years or so – then deposit-based schemes become more attractive, especially if your fund has done well in the past but you now want to make sure that it is not going to suffer from any sudden stock market drop before you retire.

— How to choose a personal plan —

As with any major financial commitment, you need to think carefully about what is on offer, and whether you can afford it, before signing up. In this section we will examine the main points to consider when choosing one of the many plans on offer.

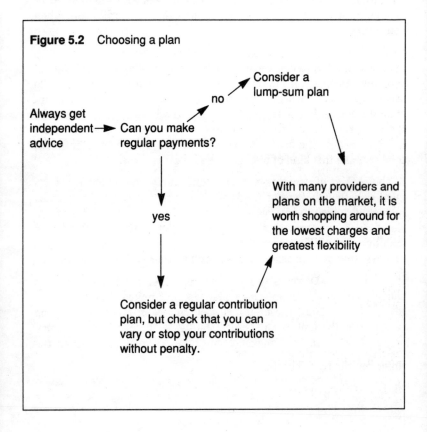

Figure 5.2 Choosing a plan

Regular contribution plans

Providers set rules for ways you can contribute to a plan; it is important to remember that these rules are made for commercial reasons, and are not decreed by the government, so if you shop around you may be able to find a plan that suits your needs better. Most providers operate regular contribution plans and single lump sum plans. Many plans set minimum amounts for contributions, both from you and from your employing company, if it is contributing to your plan. You will usually be allowed to make extra one-off contributions to regular contribution plans.

Most regular contribution plans allow you to increase your contributions at will. Some plans let you increase your payments automatically each year by a fixed amount or else by the increase in the index of National Average Earnings, published annually by the government.

You should always check that you can miss some payments to a regular contribution plan without penalty. This is important, since there may be times during your working life when you want to, or are forced to, suspend contributions for a while.

To get this flexibility, you may need to buy a 'waiver of premium' with your plan; this allows you to miss contributions if your income is reduced because you become ill or are made redundant.

Regular payment plans give you the discipline you need to make regular savings. If you are confident about your career prospects and feel that it is likely that you will have a steady income in the future, then this type of commitment makes sense.

There is a basic tension here between you and the provider; the provider will tend to want as much freedom as possible to alter the terms of the plan, in particular the charges, in the future. You, on the other hand, need to limit the provider's freedom to do this as much as you can, while giving yourself as much freedom as possible to vary contribution levels, transfer to other funds and so on. It is up to you to study the terms of the plans you are considering to find which ones offer you the best deal. In particular, look for:

● the freedom to miss some payments
● the freedom to make additional payments if you come into some money
● the freedom to reduce the amount of your payment.

Lump sum plans

These plans give you more freedom than regular contribution plans, but will often work out as more expensive to run if you take out a series of lump sum plans over the years.

Lump sum plans give you a pension based on a single, one-off payment. If you are self-employed, run a business, or do not have a regular income, then you may find that these kinds of plans are appropriate – every time you have some spare cash you can put it into a fund. Arranging your pension this ways means that you will need to be more self-disciplined at saving than with the regular contributions system.

The main disadvantages of lump sum plans are:

- Each plan is separate, and you will find that the terms available will vary over time. This means that, unlike some regular contribution plans, you can't agree to favourable terms once and for all when you begin your pension.
- If you take out a series of lump-sum plans over a number of years you will probably pay more in charges than if you had taken out a regular contribution plan.

A compromise solution might be to take out a regular contribution plan with fairly low payments, but which allows you to make extra one-off contributions when you wish. Alternatively, you could have a regular contribution plan and take out separate lump sum plans when you want to – but this method is likely to be a little more expensive.

Transferring a personal pension plan

By law, all personal plans must allow you to transfer your fund to another provider's plan if you wish; to discourage you from doing this, many plans have quite heavy penalties. These come in many forms, including:

- surrender charges, levied when you make the transfer
- loss of 'loyalty bonuses', which are only paid if you keep the plan until you retire, or, in some cases, for a shorter fixed period.

These charges are frequently high, especially if you transfer or stop your plan in the first few years. In such cases, you could even find that the fund is worth less than the amount you have paid in, or, if you stop in the first 18 months or so, that no money is returnable to you at all.

You are not forced to stick with the same plan until you retire, but make sure when you sign up for a plan that you understand exactly what the penalties are for doing so. If you feel unsure about the future, you could consider making small regular contributions to a plan, with the facility for one-off extra payments, and taking out another plan later if your earnings increase.

Your retirement age

You can choose to retire at any age between 50 and 75 with personal plans, which gives you a lot of freedom. Some providers, however, have special rules to limit this; for example, you may be asked to set a retirement date when you first take out the plan, and there may be penalties for retiring beforehand, but not later. In such cases, it would be wise to set an early retirement date, but you may be better off finding a provider that lets you set the date much nearer the time.

Early retirement is covered in detail in Chapter 8. Many people find the idea attractive, but in order for your pension to do its job, which is to give you an adequate income after you have stopped working, the fund will have to have grown to sufficient size. If you retire at, say, 52, you will have contributed less than if you retire at 65 or 75, so your fund will be smaller; at the same time, you will be expecting to receive a pension for more years in retirement. If you have been a very high earner and have built up a large fund, it may well be enough to allow you to retire early in some style, but even in this case you might be better off keeping up the contributions and 'retiring' later, in the meantime living off other earnings and savings.

The ability to choose a retirement date is the real freedom underlying personal plans, and it applies most to self-employed people and business owners. You don't have to stop work to take a pension from a personal plan, and you don't have to take the pension until 75 even if you have stopped work (assuming you can live on other earnings and savings). This means that you could, for example, start working fewer days a week but supplement your reduced income with the pension, enabling you to ease into retirement slowly. Conversely, you could carry on making money, perhaps as a consultant, until you are 75, by which time your pension fund could have grown impressively, giving you a substantially increased pension. You can increase your flexibility by having several plans with different retirement ages.

Choosing how to take the pension

Chapter 8 deals in detail with how to claim your pension on retirement, and there are many issues that you don't have to (and shouldn't) decide on until you are near retirement age.

When you first start the plan, though, check if there will be a penalty if you exercise your option to buy an annuity on the open market when you retire. The penalty may be disguised as a 'bonus' which is paid only if you buy the annuity from the original provider. This is to be avoided – as we will see in Chapter 8 the difference between the best and the worst annuity rates on offer can be as much as 30 per cent. Thus, if you bought your annuity badly, you could end up with, say, £7,000 a year instead of £10,000.

Most pensions have an open-market option written into the contract so that you can shop around like this – and you really must do it.

How does inflation affect personal pensions?

What you really want from a pension is money that you can spend in real terms. It is no good having pension income of £1,000 per month if that is the price of a cup of tea when you retire! What you want is £1,000 per month in real terms – in other words, you need a sum of money that takes inflation into account.

Unfortunately, no one knows exactly what future rates of inflation will be. It is all based on estimates.

Life assurance companies often project forward at rates of 6 per cent and 12 per cent growth. This produces astronomical pension figures for young people, so it is confusing if you are told that paying in £50 a month will produce a pension of £100,000 in 30 years' time. If inflation were to average 7 per cent per year for the next 30 years, then that £100,000 would be worth only £12,277 in today's terms.

What you should do is to ask your pension provider to give you figures based on a real rate of return of, say, 3 per cent or 4 per cent, which is generally seen as an achievable target for passive investments like pension funds. This means that you are assuming that your pension fund will grow at 3 per cent or 4 per cent more than inflation, rather than 6 per cent or 12 per cent. This will give you a better idea of what you should contribute to get an adequate pension.

Comparing providers

After deciding what type of plan you want, and the terms that fit your needs, the next step is to choose a provider. You can find out quite a lot about them and their funds from specialist magazines such as *Money Management* (see page 159).

Providers are in competition with one another for your business, and one of the main sales techniques they use to persuade you to choose them over another provider is to tell you how wonderfully their pension funds have performed. Obviously, you want your fund to perform well, because it will mean more money for you when you retire, but it is important to realise that:

1 No one, not even the professionals, has ever or can ever precisely predict the true future performance of an investment, especially over many years.
2 The past performance of investments such as pension funds are not a reliable guide to their future performance.

These two simple facts of life lie at the heart of investing, and are what make it fun. What professional investors do is make educated guesses and hedged bets about future performance, and that it what the managers of your fund will be doing, probably quite well.

As we saw on page 71, different types of funds carry different levels of risk, and to this extent the performance of broad categories of fund are roughly predictable according to their risk category – but this is as far as it goes.

Thus, while providers and advisers may lay a lot of emphasis on the past performance of their funds, you really mustn't be swayed by it. Realistically, what you can hope for is that your fund performs around the average for that category of fund over the many years it will be invested – for the mathematically inclined, this is known as 'regressing to the mean', which means that investment performance tends to become more and more like the average over time. This is no bad thing, though – the effects of your saving combined with average growth in the fund will do the job required, which is to give you a pension when you retire. Remember, your pension fund is not for gambling with – if you want to make riskier investments, do it with other money, not with your pension.

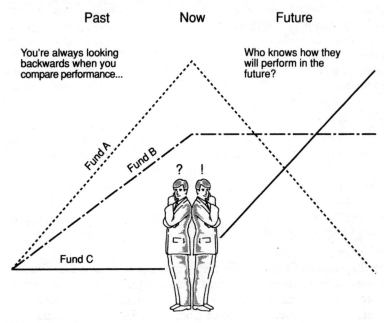

Figure 5.3

When choosing a provider, what you really need to be looking at is the nature of their company and what they are charging you. These can be broken down in the following categories.

The provider's financial strength
You'll probably need professional help to judge this properly. One way is to look at the Standard & Poor's UK life insurer financial strength ratings (ask your local reference library how to obtain this) – this rates providers according to Standard & Poor's professional opinion of their financial capacity and ability to pay out on their plans and policies.

The provider's investment philosophy
This is particularly relevant for with-profits and unitised with-profits plans, because you don't have the access to information as you do with the other types of plan. What you need to know is the degree of risk the provider takes with your fund – and they have to tell you if you ask.

The provider's charges
Most providers do not offer a fixed level of charges for the entire period of the plan, because they do not know what their expenses will be in the future. Some providers do, however, give a 'ceiling' (upper limit) beyond which the charges can't be raised. In types of plan where there are no explicit charges, it is hard to tell exactly what the expenses will be, but providers of with-profits plans must now produce a booklet with some details of the possible expenses, which is of some help.

Providers also have to publish 'reduction in yield' (RIY) figures which show you the effect of all their charges on the investment return of the plan. You will almost certainly need professional help to decipher RIY information, and you should watch out for different RIYs on different levels of contribution – usually, the lower the contribution, the higher the charges. You can also get useful tips from magazines like *Money Management* (see page 159).

Who owns the provider?
In the case of a life assurance 'office', you should check whether it is a company with shareholders or a mutual organisation owned by its investors. The smaller 'mutuals' could be vulnerable to takeovers or mergers, which could affect your plan in the future. You should also check whether the provider has a foreign owner, and how separate it is from other companies in its group, if it is part of one. Discuss the implications of this with a qualified adviser. Look for providers who are genuinely looking for new business and intend to compete in the pensions market in the future.

—— Buying a personal plan ——

Once you have read up on the pension system and have a reasonably clear idea of what's on offer and what is suitable for you, it is time to take the plunge and set about taking out a plan. This may involve much work, if you want to get a good deal, since you will have to fight your way through a lot of salesmanship to get to the bottom of any particular plan.

Much depends on who you buy the plan from. You can either go direct to the provider, or you can use an adviser. Whoever you go to, you must be careful to understand just what they will and won't tell you, and how they are remunerated. Although anyone who advises on or sells pensions is heavily regulated, if you don't take the trouble to do your own homework, the chances are that you won't get the best deal.

For this reason, it is important to understand how the Financial Services Act affects the selling of pensions (see Chapter 2). Many 'advisers' are really salespeople, and it is not easy to tell the difference at first glance – not only that, but some salespeople may actually give better advice than some advisers do! In effect, the distinction between the two has become quite blurred.

If you are already interested in the plans offered by particular providers you can get information about the plans direct from them. The telephone book may have the address and phone number of a local branch or office. If not, your local library should be able to find details of the head office for you.

Specialist magazines are a useful source of information about plans generally and of surveys comparing the different plans which are available. An added advantage is that surveys usually give details of how to contact the providers for more information.

Here's a checklist of the information you need about any plan you are considering:

- A detailed description of the plan.
- What payments are required.
- Are any of the benefits fixed? If so, which ones?
- For with-profits plans, a full description of how bonuses are calculated.
- Full details of the investment funds, if applicable.
- Is your capital (your contributions) at risk?
- Details of the transfer value of the plan in the first five years or so.
- Details of all charges and expenses. Don't expect these to be easy to follow – get an independent adviser to scrutinise them.
- Realistic examples of how the plan could work out.

'Telephone number' examples

Pension salespeople want you to take out their plan, so naturally they want to present the examples of how the plan can work in the best possible light. Often you will see examples which quote astronomical figures (sometimes called 'telephone numbers' because they have so many digits). The figures are large because they are not properly adjusted for the effects of inflation – what you need to know is what your fund will be worth in today's money.

Example

Suppose you are a man of 40 wishing to retire at 60 and draw a pension of £10,000 after tax, with that pension continuing to be paid to your wife if you die first. With annual increases of 5 per cent to help counteract inflation, you will actually need a fund of £155,000.

So, as you are 40, you have only 20 years in which to build up those funds.

Follow the simple steps below and you should reach a reasonable funding figure for your pension:

1 Decide what your target pension is in today's money – for example £10,000.
2 Have your adviser work out what this figure will be when you retire, based on your view of inflation.
3 Ask the adviser for a quotation that will produce a pension of the inflated size, assuming that the pension fund increases in value, through sound investment, at a rate of 3 per cent or 4 per cent above your chosen inflation figure.

This is nowhere near as complex as it sounds once you understand the principle, and if your pension adviser doesn't understand it, find one who does.

In any event, the table on page 86 gives examples of the amount you would need to put into a personal pension fund in order to get any worthwhile result.

Assuming that everyone wants half salary on retirement with 50 per cent to spouse on death, and also assuming that pension funds will grow at 8.5 per cent with inflation at 5.5 per cent, the following contributions are needed, expressed as a percentage of gross salary:

| | Proposed retirement age | | |
Age now	55	60	65
30	18.55%	13.58%	9.1%
35	25%	17.7%	12.69%
40	35.71%	23.58%	16.45%
45	58.13%	33.78%	22.02%

Deciding how much pension you need

This depends on a number of factors, including your age and your income.

Your age

Your age is an important factor in pension planning because it affects the question of how urgent it is for you to take out a pension.

- If you are, say, aged 55 and have little or no pension provision, you don't have many years in which to accumulate the necessary pension benefits, so planning a pension should be a top priority for you.
- If you are, say, 22, you may not have begun work yet, and pensions will be less of a priority than getting established in a career and finding somewhere to live.
- If you are a young person with a family and not much spare income, providing for your family may be a much higher priority than starting a pension.
- If you are a couple in their 40s or early 50s, on good income but still struggling with school fees and the costs of university education, you may find that it is difficult to make additional pension contributions. However, by the time you are in your 40s, there is no time to waste before taking steps to improve your pension as much as possible.

The difference between the age you are now and the age at which you want to retire gives you the length of time available in which you can contribute to a pension.

Example
If you are 30 years old and intend to retire at 65, you have 35 years in which to build a pension fund. The contribution level you should

make is much lower than for someone planning the same pension but who, being aged 45, has only 20 years in which to accumulate the necessary contributions.

Your income

Your income influences your pension in two ways:

- It determines the maximum pension you can create by law.
- It affects the amount of pension contributions which you can afford to make after paying for more pressing needs.

Since most people earn more in their 30s than in their 20s, and even more as they get closer to retirement, the limit on how much you can contribute to your pension each year increases.

Working out the figures

1 Look at your monthly expenditure budget and subtract all the items that you will no longer be spending money on once you have retired. For example, your mortgage should have been paid off, you will no longer be paying National Insurance, nor any pension contributions. You will not be travelling to work or be paying union dues. Your monthly expenditure budget in retirement should be smaller.
2 Add to your budget any increase in expenditure you can expect. For example, you may have higher heating bills if you are going to be spending more time at home, and you may use your private telephone more because you are not using the one at work. You will have more free time and may find yourself planning more holidays. As you get older it may become necessary to have DIY jobs done by professionals.
3 Once you have estimated the amount you would need if you were to retire tomorrow, then the rest is simple maths.

Example
Imagine you currently earn £20,000 a year. You might have take-home pay of £1,200 per month. You may decide that you'll be able to live on a monthly income of £700 in today's money after tax when you have retired. You may need a gross income of around £10,000 a year to achieve this, depending on your tax allowances. Your pension adviser should be able to calculate this figure for you; if your adviser can't do this, get another adviser.

It is no good planning for your pension unless you have a target. Make your pension adviser work out this target with you and make sure you understand it. Remember, if the adviser is not willing to explain and help you understand this, then you have the wrong adviser.

Final precautions

Although the Financial Services Act gives you good protection, there is an outside chance that you may be unlucky and encounter a fraudster. Here are some precautions you can take:

- Do your homework thoroughly.
- Compare advisers, providers and plans.
- Check up on advisers and providers (see Chapter 2).
- Get everything in writing.
- Make your contribution cheques out to the provider, not to the adviser.
- Keep every document and note on file.

It's your money! Make sure it is going to the right place so you can enjoy a carefree retirement – you will have earned it!

6

PENSIONS FOR COMPANY DIRECTORS AND BUSINESS OWNERS

If you are an executive or a company director, you may be able to take advantage of specialised pension schemes which are more generous than usual. They are:

- Executive pension plans (EPPs)
- Small self-administered schemes (SSAS)

— Executive pension plans (EPPs) —

Many senior executives and company directors belong to improved varieties of the main occupational scheme run by their company; these usually give improved benefits in retirement.

EPPs, which are decreasing in popularity, are an alternative. They are occupational schemes for individuals and small groups of employees, such as top executives. They are less flexible than personal pension plans, but do have some tax advantages. If you are thinking of joining an EPP, you will definitely need expert independent advice.

The tax advantages include:

- Automatic benefits for spouses and dependants.
- In some cases, all of the fund can be taken as a tax-free lump sum.
- The fund grows tax-free.
- There is full income tax relief on your contributions.
- There is full corporation tax relief on your employer's contributions.
- The maximum Death in Service benefits for your beneficiaries if

you die is currently four times your salary. Inheritance tax can be avoided if the plan is in trust.

- You can take the pension between the ages of 60 and 75, and it is taxed as income.

EPP contributions must go into funds run by insurance companies. They are final salary schemes, but your contributions are invested on a money purchase basis, which means you have your own personal fund. New restrictions are being introduced on how much employers can contribute, because in the past EPPs were popular ways of avoiding tax.

Other features include:

- You can use an EPP to contract out of Serps, although it is usually better to do this through an appropriate pension scheme.
- Some providers will offer loans against an EPP. Some members use these loans to finance business ventures.
- Many plans have substantial penalties if you retire early.

Pitfalls

It is important to get advice before joining an EPP because:

- The tax rules on EPPs are very complicated.
- The Inland Revenue is known to scrutinise the schemes very closely.
- You can be caught by unduly high commissions.
- The improved flexibility for personal plans means that they may be a better option in many cases.

__ Small self-administered schemes __ (SSAS)

If you are a director of a small company, and own 20 per cent or more of the business, you may be able to join an SSAS. Although they are primarily pension schemes, they are designed to allow the funds to be used to help finance the business.

The main features are:

- The pension is based on an average of your last three years' salary.
- The pension is taxed as income.

- You can buy the annuity up to the age of 75.
- If you die after retiring, five years' pension can be paid as a lump sum to your beneficiaries.
- There are automatic benefits for spouses and dependants.
- You can take a large tax-free lump sum. There are many conditions, but it is often about 1.5 times your final salary.
- The maximum Death in Service benefits for your beneficiaries if you die is currently four times your salary.

Using an SSAS for the business

The main advantages of an SSAS for the company are:

- The directors can use the fund to buy the company's own shares.
- The directors have flexibility over deciding when contributions are paid, and how much they will be. Limits on these are being brought in, however.
- The directors can have complete control of the administration of the scheme.
- The directors can choose how the funds are invested.
- The directors can use the funds to buy business premises, so long as the company pays commercial rents for their use. Normally the fund can't be used to buy residential property.
- The directors can use the fund to lend the company money, although the company must pay commercial rates of interest.
- The fund grows free of both income tax and capital gains tax.

Like EPPs, SSASs have been abused in the past, and are coming under increasing scrutiny and regulation by the authorities, which has the effect of making them complicated to administer. If you are a major shareholder and director of a company, you will need to consider all the issues carefully before agreeing to join such a scheme. The days when SSAS funds could be used to buy yachts and paintings by Renoir are well and truly over! Remember that the government wants SSASs to be used primarily for directors' pensions, and you must make sure that the fund can pay out pensions and benefits when they are due.

7

OPTING OUT AND SWITCHING SCHEMES

—— Contracting out of SERPS ——

As with all pension decisions, it is a good idea to get independent professional advice before making your move. A detailed description of SERPS, the State Earnings Related Pension Scheme, was given in Chapter 4. As a reminder, here are the main points:

- Unless you are a low earner, you can join SERPS, as long as you are an employee.
- The SERPS pension is based on an average of your earnings over your working life, within upper and lower earnings limits which change annually.
- SERPS may not be a good idea for everyone, especially not for younger people.
- The main advantage of SERPS is that the pension is protected against inflation both while you are working and after you have retired. However, since the government has already reduced SERPS pensions for future pensioners, and is likely to do so again, younger people may not get a good deal out of SERPS.
- If you earn less than £8,500 a year, it is usually not worthwhile opting out into an 'appropriate personal pension'. This is because the National Insurance rebate will probably not cover the pension provider's charges.
- If you are a man under 42 or a woman under 37 and you earn more than £8,500 a year, it may be worthwhile opting out.
- You can choose whether or not to contract out, unless you belong to

a contracted-out final salary scheme – in this case the employer
has made the choice for you.

● If you are in a contracted-out money purchase scheme, check if you
have the choice of opting out – some schemes allow you to stay in.

The government wants to encourage people to opt out of SERPS
because it wants to reduce its liability for paying state pensions in the
twenty-first century. In the meantime, you should think twice before
making the decision – don't automatically assume that contracting
out is right for you.

Contracting out of SERPS with final salary schemes

If you contract out of SERPS with this type of scheme, the scheme
will give you a guaranteed minimum pension (GMP) when you retire
and a guaranteed spouse's pension. Your National Insurance contributions are reduced.

The GMP will be abolished in April 1997; it is roughly equivalent to
the SERPS pension you would be entitled to. At present, you can't
lose by contracting out because the DSS will pay you the difference
between the SERPS you would have earned and the GMP you receive.
See leaflet NP46 from the DSS for further details.

It is not clear yet what, if anything, will replace the GMP.

Contracting out of SERPS with occupational money purchase schemes (COMPS)

As with final salary schemes, your National Insurance contributions
are reduced if you contract out. Your employer must pay the equivalent of your and his National Insurance rebates into your fund for
your benefit; these are called your 'protected rights'.

Whether or not you will be better off by doing this will largely depend
upon the performance of the pension fund and the annuity rate you
can buy when you retire.

COMP schemes are difficult to administrate, and many employers let
you contract out by using an appropriate personal pension instead –
this is likely to become increasingly common in the future.

Figure 7.1 Contracting out of SERPS

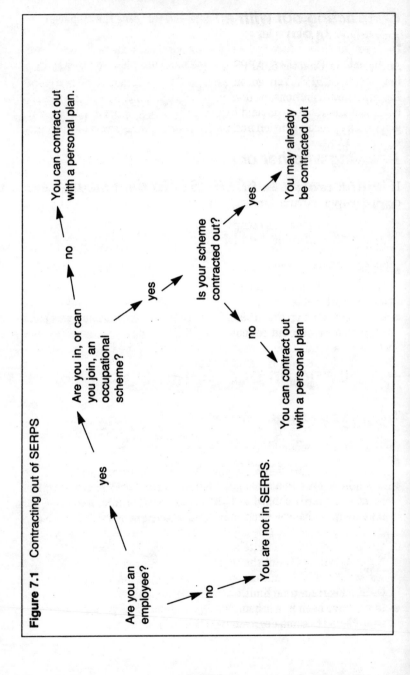

Contracting out with an appropriate personal pension (APP)

As we saw in Chapter 5, APPS are specifically designed for contracting out of SERPS. You go on paying the full amount of National Insurance contributions, as does your employer, but part of the contributions – the rebate – is paid by the DSS into your APP. APPs must give you a spouse's pension and the annuity must increase each year.

Deciding whether or not to contract out

It is worth paying a fee for independent advice on this – it does depend on your circumstances. In general, though:

- Don't leave a generous occupational scheme to contract back into SERPS. In particular, don't leave a good final salary scheme for SERPS.
- Older people have more reason to stay in SERPS if they have been relatively low earners; the pension is protected against inflation, and is predictable.
- If you are retiring after 1999, the SERPS pension has already been reduced once; it could be reduced again.

— Leaving an occupational scheme —

Transferring pension rights from an occupational scheme is one of the most controversial parts of pension planning today. Before we examine this in detail, we should look at what happens if you simply leave a scheme without joining another scheme or plan.

- If you have been in a scheme for only two years or less, the scheme is not necessarily obliged to give you any benefits at all. The scheme may give you back your contributions, or part of them, but it will depend on the rules of the particular scheme. A generous scheme may give you quite a good deal; however, the Inland Revenue will not count the refund as part of a pension deal, and will want to tax it, unless you put the money into a personal plan within a certain time limit.
- If you have been in a scheme for more than two years your pension is protected to some degree by law.

● If you are leaving a final salary scheme after two or more years, but before retiring, you are entitled to a pension, but it is based on your salary when you leave and the years you have worked. This is called a deferred pension.

Example
Joe is leaving his job after 3 years to become a musician. He has been earning £14,000 a year, but now he intends to live on state benefits until he can make a living in music, and he knows that this may take many years. Until that happens, he isn't going to join a pension scheme or plan. His scheme administrators tell him that his deferred pension will be £14,000 × 3⁄60 = £700 a year in today's money, with some protection against inflation.

● If you are leaving a money purchase scheme, the contributions you and your employer have already paid in will continue to grow until you retire.

Deferred pensions in final salary schemes

Until 1991, there was little inflation protection for deferred pensions, so if you had left a final salary scheme long before you retired, the deferred pension often became worthless. Since then, it must by law be linked to annual increases in the Retail Prices Index, up to a maximum of 5 per cent a year – this is called limited price indexation, or LPI. If inflation goes higher than this, you could suffer. Good schemes will offer you increased pensions to counteract this, and will also give you good death and dependants' benefits.

Transferring pension benefits

Almost all employees in occupational schemes will be affected by pension transfers. They will concern you unless you stay with the same employer all your working life and the employer keeps the same scheme going throughout the period. You are affected if:

● you are made redundant
● you leave a company to become self-employed
● your company is taken over and the new owners change the scheme
● you are in a public organisation which is privatised
● you have a deferred pension in an old scheme
● you move to a new company with a new scheme
● you have a personal pension which could be improved upon.

Figure 7.2 Leaving occupational schemes

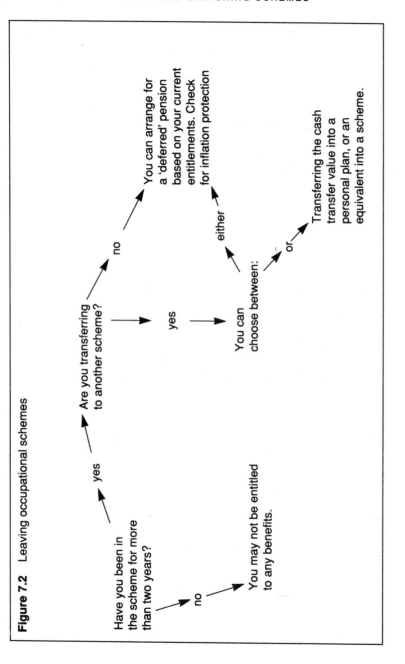

Figure 7.3 Transferring pension benefits

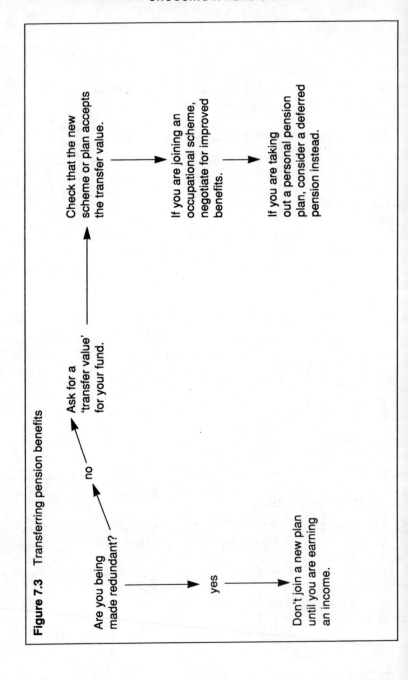

Are you being made redundant?

yes

Don't join a new plan until you are earning an income.

no

Ask for a 'transfer value' for your fund.

Check that the new scheme or plan accepts the transfer value.

If you are joining an occupational scheme, negotiate for improved benefits.

If you are taking out a personal pension plan, consider a deferred pension instead.

The pitfalls

The main pitfalls are:

- the way the transfer value is worked out
- conflicts between the rules of different schemes and plans
- the scale of charges if you join or leave a scheme.

How transfer values are worked out

If you are switching from a final pay scheme, the transfer value must be worked out by the scheme's actuary. The value of a transfer can be problematic. This is because the actuary has to convert your entitlements, based on the 'years' you have built up, into a cash figure in today's money. The idea is to give you a transfer value which would give you the same pension (if you reinvested the cash now) as you would have got from a deferred pension. In practice, however, the transfer value is calculated using an assumption of a low inflation rate, so they do not truly represent the full value of your entitlements.

Conflicts between the rules of the two schemes

Since all schemes and plans are different from one another, the scheme you are transferring from and the scheme or plan you are transferring to have to work out a compromise over the transfer value; you may be the loser in this compromise.

The problem of charges

If an insurance company is running one of the schemes or plans, your transfer money may suffer quite high charges and commissions. You will need advice to make sure you get the best deal.

Avoiding the pitfalls

You must get independent advice before arranging a transfer, and make sure that you pay for the advice by a fee, rather than by sales commissions. Many people would be better off if they didn't transfer at all, so make sure that your adviser really knows what he or she is talking about.

Transferring to an occupational scheme

If you are moving from one public sector scheme to another, there should be no problem. Most public sector schemes are in a 'transfer club', which means that the number of years' worth of benefits you have built up in the old scheme are simply transferred to the new scheme.

In the private sector, if you are transferring from one final salary scheme to another, things may not be so easy. The old scheme may tell you that you have a certain number of years-worth of entitlements built up, but the new scheme may tell you that the number is lower – perhaps half of what the old scheme tells you. This is because:

- Transfer values are lower than the true value of the benefits (see page 99).
- Your new job may well be at a better salary, and the scheme may offer better benefits. The new scheme will reduce the transfer 'years' from the old scheme to take these factors into account.

If you feel that you are losing out on such a transfer, you should first get independent advice, and then include your pension in your negotiations with your employer over your 'employment package'. You may find that your new employer will improve the transfer value in order to get you to join the company.

If you are transferring to a money purchase occupational scheme, remember to check the arrangements carefully for charges and commissions (see page 69).

If you find you are losing out

If, despite your best efforts, you still feel that you are losing out on a transfer, don't forget that you can top up your pension through an AVC or an FSAVC (see page 46).

Transferring to a personal pension

If you are in an occupational scheme, transferring to a personal plan is really a last resort. This is because you will lose many of the benefits provided by a good occupational scheme, and also because it is difficult to compare the benefits offered by a personal plan with those of a final salary scheme.

In order to compare them, you need to know:

- full details of your accrued benefits from the old scheme
- full details of AVCs in the old scheme, and if there are penalties when you transfer
- full details of the old scheme's rules on inflation protection, and death and disability benefits.

You will need the help of an independent adviser to make a proper comparison between the old scheme and the new plan.

Buy-out bonds

These are also known as 'Section 32 plans'. They are a special kind of personal pension plan for people who are transferring from an occupational scheme. You pay the transfer value from your old scheme into the plan. The money buys a 'deferred annuity', which will pay an income starting at an agreed date in the future.

You can't make any additional contributions to a buy-out bond, and you can't use it to contract out of SERPS. The advantage of a buy-out bond over a personal plan is that it retains the GMP (see page 93). As GMPs will be abolished in April 1997, this may reduce the attraction of buy-out bonds.

If you are made redundant

Unless you are going straight into another job, you should be careful about starting up a new pension straight away. If you are given a golden handshake of over £30,000 (1996 figures), it will be taxed at your highest rate, so it could be sensible to have the excess paid directly into a pension plan to avoid tax.

Some employers give generous redundancy packages. You may get advantageous terms for early retirement. This can be very worthwhile, since the best deals can significantly boost your pension, but make sure that you get advice before accepting.

Transfer checklist

Here are the main things you should do if you are transferring:

- Get independent advice on a fee basis.

- Make sure you have all the details of both the old scheme and the new one.
- If you are being made redundant, don't be in a hurry to transfer.

Stopping or switching a personal plan

This is covered in detail in Chapter 5. You should always check the penalties and charges for stopping your contributions or moving the plan before you sign up for it in the first place – some providers make these charges high, which will adversely affect the performance of your fund.

8
CLAIMING YOUR PENSION

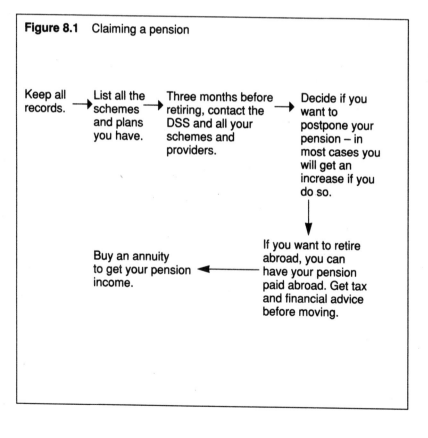

Figure 8.1 Claiming a pension

Keep all records.
→ List all the schemes and plans you have.
→ Three months before retiring, contact the DSS and all your schemes and providers.
→ Decide if you want to postpone your pension – in most cases you will get an increase if you do so.

↓

If you want to retire abroad, you can have your pension paid abroad. Get tax and financial advice before moving.
← Buy an annuity to get your pension income.

Preparing to retire

In the final year before you retire you should start getting all your paperwork in order and make contact with the various bodies who will be paying your pensions.

Here are the steps you should take:

1 Collect all the documentation relating to all your different pensions – hopefully, you will have kept every piece of paper you have received through your working life.

2 Make a list of your various pensions, and write your relevant reference numbers against each pension – for example, in the case of state pensions, you will need to quote your National Insurance number on all letters. Check to see if you have forgotten any schemes from old employers.

3 Organise all your pension papers into files. You will also need to open files for your correspondence with the various providers.

4 Write to all your pension administrators, reminding them of your impending retirement and of your intention to claim the pension. Pensions from old employers will probably take the longest to sort out, so write to them first. Remember to quote the relevant reference numbers.

5 Keep copies of all letters you send, and all the ones you receive. This will help you prove your point if there are any mistakes.

6 If you have to telephone anyone regarding your pension, use a notepad to record what is said, with the time, date and the name of the person you speak to. Preferably, use the same notepad for all calls – this way, you will have all the notes in one place.

7 When you start to receive your pensions, make sure that you file all the paperwork with the rest of the documents. When you complete your tax return you will need to refer to them.

This may all seem rather fussy, but mistakes and disputes do sometimes occur, so the more evidence you have to support your claim, the better; in addition, the more organised you appear to be, the more responsive the pension administrators are likely to be.

The tax-free lump sum

If you are entitled to a tax-free lump sum from a pension fund, you will need to decide how much you are going to take (up to the limit of approximately 25 per cent) and what you are going to do with it. Your decision will depend on your individual circumstances, but here are the main possibilities. You can:

- spend it
- pay off any outstanding mortgage on your home
- invest it
- use it to buy an annuity.

As people get older, they naturally become more conservative about their money, because they know that if they get into financial difficulties they may not have the energy to put things right. On the other hand, if you find that you are well provided for, you may feel that some of the lump sum would be best spent on things that give you pleasure. It's a personal matter – by the time you retire, you will have acquired the life experience to make a sensible decision.

If you still have a mortgage outstanding, it is usually a good idea to use the lump sum to pay it off – this will substantially reduce your outgoings, and give you the security of knowing that you own your home in full. As with all financial decisions, you should get advice before doing this, since in some cases there may be financial penalties for early repayment, and factors such as the current rate of inflation and the rate of interest on your loan will affect your timing.

If you are interested in investment, your retirement will give you plenty of time to work at it. Some retired people take up most of their time with investment activity – and the lump sum gives them capital to do this with, although in most cases they will already have other investment capital.

If you find that taking the lump sum will leave you with a smaller pension than you need, you could use it to buy an annuity (see page 112).

When you decide how much to take, bear in mind that it is usually worth taking the maximum, since it is tax free – your pension, remember, is taxable as income. Pay an independent adviser for an opinion on what you should do.

——— Claiming state pensions ———

As we saw in Chapter 3, the DSS should send you form BR1 about three months before you reach state pension age, together with a letter telling you what state benefits you will receive. If it doesn't arrive, contact your local DSS.

The main points to bear in mind when claiming are:

- Make sure that you claim in good time since the DSS will not backdate any claims for more than 12 months, and, in the case of claims for dependants, not more than 6 months.
- Always quote your National Insurance number on all letters to the DSS.
- If you think that the DSS has made a mistake in your assessment, write to your local office asking for a full explanation of how your pension has been assessed. Use their reply as a basis for complaint if you believe that they are wrong.

The pension payment

At present, you have some choice over how you can receive your state pension:

- It can be paid weekly using an 'order book'.
- It can be paid directly in a bank or building society account either monthly or quarterly.

Order books contain dated payment slips which you can cash at a Post Office – you have to nominate which branch. You can't cash your weekly pension before it is due, but you can cash it up to three months later. If you haven't cashed it in by then, you should contact the DSS and arrange for payment. The pension week starts on a Sunday, so usually the first day you can collect your pension is on the following Monday. You can arrange for someone else to collect your pension for you, but always make sure that you get the pension book back afterwards.

If you decide to have the pension paid direct into your account, you will need to fill in a special form in the DSS Leaflet NI105. Although it is convenient not to have to go to a Post Office to get the money, the disadvantage of this payment method is that the pension is paid at the end of the period, not at the beginning. If maintaining a good cashflow is important to you, you should opt for the weekly payment method.

After you have started claiming, remember that:

- You should keep records of your pension receipts for your tax return.
- You must tell the DSS about any changes to your legal status – for example, if your spouse dies, or you get divorced.
- If the DSS overpays you, it will want the money back.
- If you go into hospital for a long time, or into a home, your pension may be reduced.

You can postpone your pension

At present, you can defer your state pension by up to five years, which has the effect of increasing the amount when you claim. This works out at 7.5% extra pension for each complete year you wait.

There are some conditions:

- You can't do this if you have retired abroad.
- If your spouse is claiming a pension based on your National Insurance record, he or she must agree to the deferment as well.
- You can't backdate a deferment.
- If you defer the pension and then start to claim within the five years, you can't defer for a second time.

To arrange for the deferment, you should write to the DSS and obtain confirmation of the arrangement.

Early retirement

You cannot claim state pension before the state retirement age. If you stop work because of ill health, you may be eligible for state benefits such as the invalidity benefit. Contact the DSS for details.

If you retire abroad

If you decide to live abroad, the DSS will pay state pensions and widow's benefits to any country in the world.

There is one main drawback: the annual increases in the benefits will not be paid unless you are living in certain countries – these include the United States, EU member states, some Caribbean countries and some Commonwealth countries. For a full list, contact the DSS. If you live in a country which is not on the list, your pension will be whittled away by inflation. If you come back to the United Kingdom, though, the pension will be increased to the current rate.

If you go away for less than three months you can simply collect your pension when you come back. For longer trips, up to a maximum of two years, you can arrange to collect the pension in a lump when you come back, or you can have the money transferred overseas – remember, though, that bank charges and exchange rates can eat into your pension if you do this.

— Claiming occupational pensions —

As with the state pensions, you should expect to hear form occupational schemes by the last quarter (three months) before you retire, and if you haven't heard from them you should write to them. Most schemes will be efficiently run, but some aren't, so make sure, as with all dealings where money is involved, that you keep copies of all the paperwork and keep notes of all telephone calls.

You will find that your scheme has its own particular procedures for pension claims; here we will look at the main things you should do:

- One good tip is to arrange to go to see the pensions administrator; he or she will be able to explain your position to you and answer your questions.
- Always quote the relevant reference numbers when you write or telephone the scheme.

You need to know:

- How much pension you will get.
- How much is the maximum lump sum that you can take?
- If you take the lump sum, how much it will reduce your pension by?
- What your choices are over the way the pension is paid?
- Is there a dependant's pension if you die? If so, how much?
- Is there a spouse's pension? How much is it and will it affect your retirement pension?

The pension payment

Your pension will be paid either by the scheme itself, or by an insurance company – this depends on the type of scheme you are in. Each scheme will have its own rules on increase and payment methods, but it is usual to get the pension paid monthly in advance. As a general rule, if you have a choice of how frequently the money is paid, go for the most frequent period allowed.

Early retirement

Although there are various Inland Revenue limits on the maximum pension you can receive if you retire early, in practice most schemes will have lower maximum limits of their own. Some schemes give better terms if your employer has asked you to retire early.

You are allowed to take a guaranteed minimum pension (GMP) from a final pay scheme before the state retirement age, but only if the pension is not less than the pension you would get if it began at the state retirement age. (See page 93 for more on GMPs.)

'Protected rights pensions' cannot be paid before the state retirement age.

If you retire because of ill health

You will need to check the scheme's rules – not all schemes pay an ill-health pension, and those that do have quite complicated rules. It is in your interests to apply for this pension before you leave work, if you can.

The scheme will want proper proof of your ill health, and may require you to be examined by a doctor of its choice.

It's a good idea to look into the ill-health rules of your scheme thoroughly when you first join – the last thing you want to do if you are really ill is to have to try to work out if you can claim.

Late retirement

Check your scheme rules to see if you can postpone claiming your pension, and if it will be increased by doing so. Make sure that it is worthwhile to postpone it, and then confirm the arrangement with the scheme.

Tracking down old schemes

Sometimes it is difficult to find a pension scheme run by an old employer. In such cases, you can contact the Registrar of Pension Schemes; all schemes must be listed with the Registry by law. The address is on page 158.

If you can claim a preserved pension from an old scheme, you must check the paperwork for the address of the administrator, who will either be an insurance company or the old scheme. When you make contact, ask:

● the value of the pension
● if there are other benefits
● how the pension is paid.

Claiming AVCs and FSAVCs

In the case of AVCs, contact your employer's scheme. The administrator will tell you how much the fund is worth and how to use it to improve your pension.

FSAVCs are more complex – you will need to contact both your employer's scheme and the organisation running the FSAVC in order to claim.

———— Personal pensions ————

As with other pensions, make sure that you make contact with your provider about three months before you retire. Unless you have agreed a retirement date with the provider, you will need to let them know of your intentions.

In certain professions, such as in some sports, you are legally allowed to retire earlier than the normal age of 50. Contact the Inland Revenue for a full list of these professions.

Otherwise, you can choose the age at which you claim as long as it is between 50 and 75, subject to the rules of your plan. Remember that you can go on working after you start claiming a personal pension.

Always quote the relevant reference numbers when you write or telephone the provider. You will normally not have to buy an annuity from the provider.

The main things you need to know are:

- What is the single value of the pension fund?
- What is the value of the pension the provider offers?
- Is there a dependant's pension if you die? If so, how much?
- Is there a spouse's pension? How much is it and will it affect your retirement pension?
- Is it possible to take a lower pension in the early years and get an increased pension later? What are the figures?
- How much is the maximum lump sum you can take?
- If you take the lump sum, how much will it reduce your pension by?
- What are your choices over the way the pension is paid?
- Are there other options?

The pension payment

Normally you can choose whether to have the pension paid directly into your bank or building society account, or to be sent a cheque. Some providers also give you a choice over the frequency of the pension payment – but it is usually not more frequent than once a month – and some providers will increase the pension slightly if you agree to have it paid quarterly or annually.

You can choose to take a small pension (worth a few hundred pounds a year) as a lump sum when you retire, but this may be taxable.

Protected rights

If you have a protected rights pension from a personal plan which is contracted out, they may be separated from your main plan. You don't have to buy an annuity from the provider unless you choose to, but you will not be able to claim the pension until the state retirement age.

Choosing when to take your pension

Normally you can choose when you take your pension, as long as it is between the ages of 50 and 75. If you take your pension early, the annuity you must buy will give you a lower income because you will be receiving it for more years than if you retired later. As we will see in the section on annuities below, annuity rates change a lot from year to year, so it may be worth waiting a year or two to get a better rate – get advice on this when you are ready to retire.

Early retirement because of ill health or disability

If you have to retire because of ill health, you can start to take a pension from a personal plan whatever your age. You will need to prove that your illness meets the provider's conditions in order to claim.

Retiring early will mean that your plan will be smaller than otherwise, since you will have paid in less and it will have had less time to grow. In addition, the annuity you buy will be smaller, too, because you will be expected to live longer. To counteract this, you can purchase insurance when you take out the plan (but not after you have become ill).

—————————— Annuities ——————————

All money purchase pension schemes require you to buy an annuity when you retire. Money purchase schemes include:

- personal pension plans
- most AVCs
- most FSAVCs
- COMPS
- EPPs.

In most cases, you will have an 'open market option', which means that you don't have to buy the annuity from the provider – you can shop around to get the best rate. This is an important issue, and is covered on page 115.

In addition, if you have a personal pension, you can delay buying the annuity up to the age of 75. The government may extend this rule to cover occupational schemes in the future.

For many people, buying their annuity will be the biggest investment of their lives. It is an important matter. You have saved for years for your retirement, and you must make sure you get the best deal you can, otherwise much of your efforts will have gone to waste.

Annuities are a complicated and mysterious matter, even to many independent financial advisers. You must get the best advice you can, and be prepared to pay a reasonable fee for the guidance.

How annuities work

An annuity is a bet that you make with an insurance company. You pay your pension fund over to the company, and in return they promise to pay you a regular income, either for the rest of your life or for a certain number of years. When you die, the insurance company doesn't have to pay out any more money, and keeps the fund.

The bet you are making is that you will live longer than the insurance company thinks you will. Insurers use 'mortality tables' to work out how long it thinks you are likely to live, and if you live longer than that it will have to go on paying you your pension. Below are the main factors that insurers use to work out the rate of pension they will offer you.

Your sex
Women live several years longer than men, on average, so if you are a woman you will be offered a lower annuity rate than a man of the same age will be. There are exceptions, though; appropriate personal pension annuities must not distinguish between the sexes, and it is likely that 'unisex' annuities will become more widespread in the future.

Your health
If you have a serious illness and can prove it, some insurers will offer you a much better annuity rate because they expect you to die sooner than the average person would.

Where does the money go?

Insurers normally invest the pension fund money in fixed-interest investments, known as 'stocks' or 'bonds'. The safest of these are sold

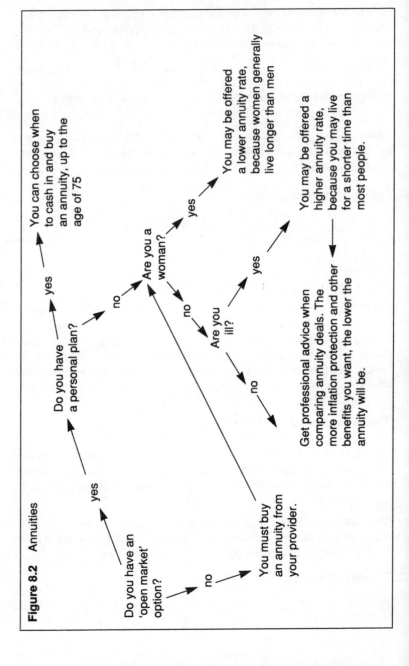

Figure 8.2 Annuities

Do you have an 'open market' option?
— yes →
— no → You must buy an annuity from your provider.

Do you have a personal plan?
— yes → You can choose when to cash in and buy an annuity, up to the age of 75
— no →

Are you a woman?
— yes → You may be offered a lower annuity rate, because women generally live longer than men
— no →

Are you ill?
— yes → You may be offered a higher annuity rate, because you may live for a shorter time than most people.
— no →

Get professional advice when comparing annuity deals. The more inflation protection and other benefits you want, the lower the annuity will be.

— 114 —

by the government, and are known as 'gilts'. Most annuity money goes into 'gilts', which pay a fixed rate of interest. The interest rates available at any particular time vary, however, and this will directly affect the annuity rate insurers will offer you.

The open market option

If you have an 'open market option', it makes sense to use it – it simply means that you can shop around for the best deals when you buy the annuity. The difference between the best and worst deals on the market is about 25 per cent. You may find though, that your provider imposes a penalty if you exercise the option, leaving you with less money in the pension fund with which to buy the annuity. If you haven't already joined a scheme, you should investigate these penalties thoroughly before making your choice.

Annuity choices

There are several types of annuity, which are covered in the next section. In addition, you have several choices to make once you have selected the type of annuity you want.

Guaranteed annuity
If you die within a few years of buying the annuity – usually five years, but sometimes longer – the insurance company will pay back the balance of your pension fund to your beneficiaries. In return for this promise you will get a reduced pension.

Payment timing
You can usually choose how often you want to receive your annuity payments, ranging from monthly to annually. If you want the money to be paid in advance (i.e. at the beginning of the period) you will normally receive a lower payment than if you agree to the annuity being paid 'in arrears' (i.e. at the end of the period).

Escalation
You can protect the effects of inflation to some extent by arranging for your annuity to be increased by a fixed percentage each year.

Proportion
If you receive your annuity in arrears and choose the 'with proportion' option, the insurance company promises to pay your beneficiaries a

proportion of the next annuity payment you would have received if you hadn't died. This option will reduce your annuity income by a small amount.

Joint life
This option is where the company promises to continue to pay all or part of the annuity to your spouse or partner if you die. In return, you accept a reduced payment.

Combinations
If you want several of these options, you can have them, but you will find that your annuity income is substantially reduced.

The most 'expensive' of these options, in terms of how much they are likely to reduce the amount of the annuity by, are joint life and escalation. Remember that most of these options simply represent variations on the bet you are making with the insurance company.

Types of annuity

The main types are:

- fixed
- increasing
- RPI-linked
- investment linked
- income drawdown.

Fixed annuities

This is the conventional, old-fashioned annuity where the amount of regular income you receive is fixed for life. Of all the annuity types, it offers the biggest income at the beginning, but inflation can eat away at its value over the years.

Example
Wendy retires at 60 and buys an annuity which gives her an income of £10,000 a year. If inflation averages at 5 per cent over the next 15 years (which is a fairly low figure), by the time she is 75 her £10,000 annual income will have the buying power of £4,800.

If she has her own home, it may well have increased in value during the same period, but she may not be willing to sell her home or to borrow against it when she is 75. If she has other investments which keep pace with inflation, these will compensate for the reduced value of the annuity, but if she doesn't, she will have to live on a substantially reduced income.

As we will see in Chapter 10, this is the main reason why it is advisable to save in other ways for your old age, in addition to your pension contributions.

Increasing annuities

To counteract the danger of inflation, you can buy an increasing annuity, where your annual income increases by a fixed rate which you agree at the outset. This makes sense, but it will mean that the annuity will be lower in the first place.

Example
Wendy retires at 60, and instead of buying a fixed annuity giving her an income of £10,000 a year, she buys an annuity that increases at 5 per cent a year. The best deal she can find at the time offers her an annual income of only £7,000. In terms of the total money the insurer pays out, she will be winning if she lives longer than the age of 75. In the meantime, she has accepted a lower income in return for increased security.

RPI-linked annuities

If you are concerned about the effects of inflation and you expect to live for a long time, the obvious answer is to buy an annuity that is directly linked to a standard inflation measure such as the Retail Prices Index (RPI). Unfortunately, they are quite hard to find, and can be expensive. To find what is on offer, go to a good independent adviser.

Example
Wendy retires at 60 and buys an RPI-linked annuity. The best deal she can find at the time offers her an annual income of £7,000, as against an income of £10,000 which she could have got by buying a fixed annuity. The longer she lives, and the higher inflation goes, the better she does out of the arrangement.

Investment-linked annuities

These are special annuities that can protect against inflation by a unit-linked or with-profits fund. They are complicated, and you will need expert advice to decide whether they are appropriate for you. In essence, you are taking on more risk, because the amount of annuity will go up or down according to the performance of the investment. In general, you should consider this type of plan only if you have substantial assets outside your pension fund.

With-profits annuities give you a low level of guaranteed basic income, with possible additional annual bonuses. Unit-linked annuities promise to pay you a certain number of units each year, but the value of those units will vary.

Income drawdown annuities

The main features of this type are:

- You take your tax-free cash lump sum at the beginning of the plan.
- The rest of your money is invested to give you an income, which will be variable.
- You have a degree of control over the investment.
- When you are 75 you must buy one of the other types of annuity with the fund.
- The plan is risky – the fund could run out before you die.
- The costs can be high.

As with investment-linked annuities, you will need expert advice before investing in this type of plan, and, unless you are fairly wealthy, they are probably not a good idea.

Shopping for an annuity

Annuities are not flexible investments; once you have signed up, you can't change your mind. Although the trend is for insurance companies to come up with ever more complicated products that are designed to give you more flexibility, insurance and investment is never a harmonious mix – and the charges for these products can be high. For most people, the best answer is to buy one of the following types where the cash payments are guaranteed:

- fixed annuities
- increasing annuities
- RPI-linked annuities.

Annuities checklist

- Shop around – at any time the difference between good and bad offers can be as much as 25 per cent.
- Annuity rates change – get expert advice on whether they are likely to go up in the short term, and buy then.
- Check for penalties on your pension fund if you exercise your open-market option.
- Be vary of overcomplicated, new fangled schemes. They could be expensive and risky.
- Consider the extra choices you have, such as 'escalation' and 'proportion' (see page 115). In particular, some degree of protection against inflation is probably a good idea.

9

HOW YOUR
PENSION IS TAXED

After you have retired, the pensions you receive are regarded as income for the UK tax purposes as long as you are resident in the United Kingdom. The main exception to this is the tax-free lump sum that you are allowed to take if you wish on retirement, but it is quite possible that a future government will phase out or abolish this perk, so, unfortunately, you can't count on it.

Income tax rates and allowances 1995/96

There are 'bands' of income tax rates, also known as 'marginal' rates, which are a relatively new invention and are liable to change in the future.

Taxable income (after deduction of allowances)	Rate	Total tax
First £3,200	20%	£640
Next £21,100	25%	£5,275
Over £24,300	40%	

If you are a UK resident (but not necessarily if you are not a UK resident) you will not have to pay income tax on all your income. This is because you are granted allowances, which means that a certain amount of income in each tax year will not be subject to tax.

The table below lists the more common personal income tax allowances. You will find the figures printed in many magazines and tax tables, and usually in newspapers after the Chancellor of the Exchequer makes the annual budget statement (the Budget). The Chancellor usually changes the personal allowances each year by increasing them roughly in line with inflation. You need to keep up to date with changes to these amounts:

The principal income tax allowance for 1995/96

Personal allowance	£3,525
Married couple's allowance	£1,720
Additional personal allowance	£1,720
Widow's bereavement allowance	£1,720
Age allowance (age 65–74)	£4,630
Married couple's allowance (age 65–74)	£2,995
Age allowance (75 or over)	£4,800
Married couple's allowance (aged 75 or over)	£3,035

Note that age allowances are reduced by £1 for every £2 of income over £14,600, but are not reduced below the personal allowance.

The lower rate of tax

Suppose you are a single woman aged 65 with an income of £6,000 in 1995/96. How much tax will you pay?

1 Your age allowance is £4,630.
 £6,000 – £4,630 = £1,640 taxable income.
2 The first £3,200 of taxable income is taxed at 20 per cent. You have £1,640 of taxable income, so your tax will be £328.

The basic rate of tax

Suppose you are a single woman aged 65 with an income of £11,525 in 1995/96. How much tax will you pay?

1 Your age allowance is £4,630.
 £11,525 – £4,630 = £6,895 taxable income.
2 The first £3,200 of taxable interest is taxed at 20 per cent = £640.
3 The balance of your taxable income will be taxed at 25 per cent;
 £6,895 – £3,200 = £3,695
 25 per cent of £3,695 is £923.75.
4 Adding the results of 2 and 3 together, we get:

	Tax
£3,200 taxed at 20 per cent =	£640
£3,695 taxed at 25 per cent =	£923.75
£6,895 = total taxable income	£1,563.75 = total tax

On your income of £11, 525 you must pay £1,563.75 income tax.

The higher rate of tax

Many people do not earn enough to be liable for tax in the 40 per cent band (which is over £27,825 in 1995/96 for a single person). Let's suppose, though, that you are a single woman aged 65 with an income of £32,525 in 1995/96. How much tax will you pay?

1 Your age allowance is £4,630, but it is reduced by £1 for every £2 of income over £14,600. Your income of £32,525 – £14,600 = £17,925, so the age allowance is theoretically wiped out. Instead of the age allowance, you claim the ordinary personal allowance of £3,525.
 £32,525 – £3, 525 = £29,000 taxable income.
2 The first £3,200 of taxable income is taxed at 20 per cent = £640.
3 The next £21,100 of your taxable income will be taxed at 25 per cent = £5,275.
4 The balance of your taxable income will be taxed at 40 per cent; this balance is:
 £29,000 – (£3,200 + £21,100) = £4,700
 40 per cent of £4,700 is £1,880.
5 Adding the results of 2, 3 and 4 together, we get:

	Tax
£3,200 taxed at 20 per cent =	£640
£21,100 taxed at 25 per cent =	£5,275
£4,700 taxed at 40 per cent =	£1,800
£29,000 = total taxable income	£7,715 = total tax

On your income of £32,525 you must pay £7,715 in income tax.

The married couple's allowance

If you are married, each spouse can earn up to their own personal allowance or age allowance tax free. In addition, as a married couple you can earn a further sum tax free – the amount depends on your age (see page 121).

Since April 1993, at your choice, you can either choose to have the married couple's allowance claimed by one of you, or it can be divided equally between you. Thus, if in any particular tax year you or your spouse has not earned enough income to use the part of the married couple's allowance allocated, it can be transferred to the other spouse. Relief on the married couple's allowance is 15 per cent for 1995/96, so it is no longer a true deduction from income.

Example

Suppose you are a married couple both aged 65. The man earns £5,000 a year, and the woman earns £15,000 a year.

	Man	**Woman**
Income	£5,000	£15,000
Less age allowance	£4,630	£4,630
Subtotal	£370	£10,370

Now you can decide what to do with the married couple's allowance; in this case it would be sensible for the woman to claim the whole of the married couple's allowance, since the man's tax liability is very small (20 per cent of £370 = £74).

	Woman
Subtotal	£10,370
Less married couples' allowance	£2,995
Taxable income	£7,375

Remember that the married couple's allowance gives 15 per cent relief, not 20 per cent relief as with the rest of the taxable income.

If you do not use the whole of your allowance in any particular year, the difference can NOT be carried forward to another year – you have lost it forever. For this reason, it is important to get your claim right.

The widow's bereavement allowance

This is an additional allowance granted, if you are a widow, in the tax year of your husband's death and in the following tax year. There is no similar allowance for husbands, although in the tax year of their wife's death they will still be granted for the full married couple's allowance. This does not continue into the following year. Thus if the husband had died in August 1993, his estate (assets) would still be granted the full offset against his taxable income before his date of death.

His wife would also, in that year, get a personal allowance and the widow's bereavement allowance (which is equivalent to the married couple's allowance), increasing her total personal allowances. This also applies in the following tax year, but after that the additional allowance will cease.

If the widow also has dependent children, she can claim the additional personal relief for children.

Relief on both of these allowances is 15 per cent for 1995/96.

How the tax is paid

At present, the system works like this:

- The basic state pension may or may not be paid with tax deducted, depending on whether or not you are still in the PAYE system.
- A pension from an occupational scheme will usually be paid with the tax already deducted through the PAYE system.
- If you have a personal pension, the pension provider will usually deduct tax through PAYE before paying you the pension.

Self-assessment

The UK tax system is being changed to a 'self-assessment' system, which is supposed to be simpler. The first self-assessment returns will be sent out in April 1997; you will be required to fill in the figures yourself, and then either:

- work out your own tax assessment and return the form by 31 January 1998, or
- return the form by the end of September 1997 and let the Inland Revenue work out your assessment.

The major difference with self-assessment is that taxpayers will be required to keep more records than they did before. From April 1996, you should start keeping such records as:

- P60, P160, P11D, P9D, P2 and P2K and P45 forms
- payslips and pay statements
- notes of tips and gratuities
- certificates for 'Taxed Award' schemes
- pension certificates and statements
- any details you have received from the Benefits Agency and the Employment Services Agency relating to state benefits and pensions.
- bank and building society statements, chequebooks and passbooks
- interest statements from other investments
- tax deduction certificates from your bank
- vouchers and statements relating to unit trusts you own
- all information of shares you buy, own or sell
- life insurance chargeable event certificates
- details of income you receive from a trust.

In short, you must keep full records relating to any financial transactions or commitments. The Inland Revenue say that you have to keep these records for only 22 months after the end of the relevant tax year, but it makes sense to keep your records for much longer than this, particularly if your affairs are complex.

Retiring abroad

Why spend your retirement in rainy Britain when you could be living in the sun? That's the way many people feel, and who can blame them? It can be done successfully – the more money you have, the better – but there are major risks, so anyone thinking of retiring abroad should appreciate that it is a serious business requiring careful long-term planning. If you want to retire abroad, the time to start planning for it is now, whatever your age.

To understand why you need to be careful, consider the financial risks:

- You will be dealing with two or more countries' taxation systems, none of which properly intermesh.
- International tax agreements that are in force now can be changed in the future.
- Some countries lure wealthy retirees in to settle, and then raise the taxes on foreigners. One favourite way is to suddenly increase inheritance taxes on foreign-owned property, so that when the retired person dies, much of the value of the property goes to the state.
- Some countries have inadequate banking systems.
- Fluctuations in inflation rates and exchange rates could reduce the buying power of your income.
- There is no certainty that political federations such as the EU will last your whole lifetime.
- British Embassies abroad are not helpful to British people in trouble.

In short, retiring abroad permanently is a challenge; if you can rise to it, you could be rewarded with a very happy retirement. What you can't do is retire abroad assuming that everything will work out by itself – it is up to you to make sure that your finances are secure.

There is another option, though. You can simply go abroad for long holidays, knowing that you can return to the United Kingdom if you need to – this generally has the effect of keeping you within the UK welfare system. If this is all you plan to do, you need not read beyond the next section.

Tax on your pension if you go abroad on holiday

As we saw in Chapter 8, your pensions can be paid abroad, or, in many cases, they can be left in the United Kingdom to accumulate until you return. As long as you are away for only short periods – as a rule of thumb, under three months – you should be classed as a tourist in the foreign country, and still pay UK tax on your pensions in the normal way. With careful planning, this can be made into quite a useful loophole – as long as the foreign country thinks of you as a tourist, it will not try to tax you. If, however, you buy property or start to bring your savings into the country, you may well become subject to foreign taxes.

Who is liable to UK taxation?

This may seem to be a strange question – but if you are planning to retire abroad, you may not be liable to UK tax. It all depends on your circumstances, and on three curious definitions invented by the taxman:

- residence
- ordinary residence
- domicile.

Residence

You may be regarded as being resident in the United Kingdom in any tax year in which you are present in the United Kingdom for at least part of the time. Anyone staying in the United Kingdom for at least six months in any year will always be regarded as being a UK resident for that tax year, and, depending on the individual's circumstances, the required period could be much less than six months.

Most other countries have similar rules to these, so it is possible for someone to be regarded as being resident in more than one country in any one tax year.

Ordinary residence

'Ordinary residence' is a strange notion, quite distinct from residence. It is the main criterion for Capital Gains Tax (CGT), and so is not directly relevant to the taxation of pensions. You can be resident in more than one country at the same time, but 'ordinarily resident' in only one country at a time.

Domicile

Domicile is another strange notion, quite distinct from residence or ordinary residence. If you are not domiciled in the United Kingdom, you are not liable for tax except on the money that you bring into the country. There are two kinds of domicile:

- domicile of origin
- domicile of choice.

Your domicile of origin is usually the country where your father was domiciled when you were born. If you have a domicile of origin outside the United Kingdom, you may be able to live in the United Kingdom for a long time without ever having to pay UK tax.

Domicile of choice is more tricky; you have to be resident in a country and have 'the intention of permanent or indefinite residence' there. If you want to change from a UK domicile, you must intend never to return for anything more than brief, infrequent visits, or the Inland Revenue will say that you haven't changed your domicile.

Each of these descriptions is used to assess whether or not you will be subject to UK taxation, or to the tax rules of another country.

What is the difference between tax avoidance and tax evasion?

Tax avoidance is when you make efforts to legally reduce or avoid paying tax by exploiting the complexity of the rules. Tax evasion is exactly the same thing, except that you break the law. The right to avoid tax is well established and, to paraphrase Lord Clyde's comments in a famous tax case of 1929, a person does nothing wrong by arranging his or her affairs to take advantage of the rules, so long as they are not broken.

The extraordinary complexity of tax legislation means that, in practice, there are many circumstances in which a layman could not possibly tell the difference between avoidance and evasion. Nevertheless, you should make sure that you do everything you can to stay within the law.

The Ramsay doctrine

The Ramsay doctrine is a set of principles in dealing with tax avoidance. It sets out the rule that when making arrangements to reduce tax, no artificial steps can be taken. This means that you can take no steps where the primary motive overall is to avoid tax. However, you can avoid the doctrine if you arrange the steps so that either they are not under your control the whole time, or that someone else receives a partial benefit from them during part of the sequence. You will need the help of a tax adviser to do this.

What if I have close connections with other countries?

If you are not a UK national, or you have a spouse who is not, or you are planning to work abroad, you should get specialist advice from a tax lawyer. You may find that you are in a position to save tax.

Tax planners' tactics

For well-to-do people, the principal worry is not Income Tax but Inheritance Tax (IHT), and Capital Gains Tax (CGT). Many people avoid IHT in the UK by getting their assets out of the country before death, which may also be beneficial when it comes to receiving state health benefits.

Really good tax lawyers can be worth their fees; the reality of the British tax regime is that the Inland Revenue's interpretation of the laws is not always the same as that of the courts, and although a prolonged court battle may cost more than it is worth, if enough money is involved it may be worthwhile in making IHT avoidance plans with this contingency in mind.

Double taxation treaties

A double taxation treaty is an agreement between two states designed to mitigate the effects of tax on people and companies that do business in both countries. If two countries do have a treaty, income arising in one country may be taxed there under a withholding tax rule, and then taxed again when it arrives in another country. There is great variation in the details of different treaties.

Strong trading countries like the United Kingdom have superior bargaining power and are generally able to force agreements which are favourable to them. Treaties may exempt withholding tax entirely from income going abroad, or they may mitigate it. In general, no country will collect another country's taxes or enforce another country's tax regulations.

Individuals are rarely extradited for tax evasion in a foreign country, although it does occur.

How UK residents are taxed on unearned income

'Unearned' income is money you receive from investments such as stocks, shares, unit trusts, and rents on property you own. It may not seem 'unearned' to you, but that is what it is called.

If you have unearned income from investments held in another country which does not have a double taxation treaty with the United Kingdom, you could be taxed twice. Remember, though, that most developed countries do have double taxation treaties with each other.

Suppose you received 'unearned' income from investments in France. Because of the double taxation treaty between the United Kingdom and France, the foreign country (in this case France) will usually forego the right to tax the income, which will then be liable to UK taxation just as if that income had arisen in this country.

It is important to note that the taxation on the income earned abroad by UK residents is paid when the income is earned or credited and not only when or if the money is returned to the United Kingdom.

Tax havens and offshore centres

'Tax haven' is a much abused term. Not all low-tax countries like to be called tax havens, and although even professionals use the name, it is not a precise one. Switzerland, for example, is not a low-tax country, but its sophisticated banking facilities and tradition of conservatism and confidentiality makes it attractive as a place for the wealthy to retire.

Some tax havens specialise in the forming of offshore companies, while others have highly developed banking facilities. Most of them are small countries (quite a number are islands), and look to offshore business as an important part of their economies, but none of them can afford to pull up the drawbridge entirely – not only are they in strong competition with one another, but also they are dependent in varying degrees on the policies and practices of the dominant trading nations of the world. Most of the money going into tax havens comes from big trading countries like the United Kingdom, all of which take steps to limit the flow of these transactions, and tax havens must take this fact into account when designing their own laws.

Although it is a principle of international law that every sovereign nation must regulate its own economy, and can set its own tax rates, so the right of a country to become a tax haven is well established, there are bureaucratic and ideological forces who would wish that such anomalies did not exist.

Even in the EU, where attempts are being made to harmonise taxation in member states, there have been no moves to set universal standards for personal taxation because of the enormous legal difficulties in doing so.

For nationals of EU countries, the offshore jurisdictions which are physically close to the EU and have special tax arrangements with the community, offer benefits which are not available at home.

If you are intrigued by tax havens and want to investigate them further, it is worth visiting them in person; detailed information is easier and cheaper to get on the spot rather than going to consultants in other countries, and many schemes and wrinkles cannot be advertised in the countries where they are of the most interest. Remember that many countries, including the United Kingdom, don't tax money earned and held abroad unless it is 'repatriated', so if you spend income from your overseas assets abroad you may not need to move to a tax haven.

10
THE FUTURE

– Why are pensions so complicated? –

If you have read this far in this book, it should be clear that the pensions industry is vast. In total, pension funds own about a third of all the companies in the United Kingdom, and the industry employs thousands of people – administrators, trustees, actuaries, advisers, lawyers, investment managers, salespeople and office staff – just to look after our retirement money. The pension funds have enormous economic power, and, as any stockbroker will tell you, they are not afraid to use it to influence how large companies are run.

Perhaps this is no bad thing. It gives our economy a degree of stability. But it also means that the pensions industry has a 'vested interest' in making sure that it remains as powerful as it is today. The government also has a vested interest – it wants to make sure that, among other things, it won't go bust in the next century paying out state pensions to the much larger number of people who will be entering retirement then. It also wants to make sure that elderly people have enough to live on. This is nothing to do with party politics – it is simply a fact of life.

Many elderly people will tell you that they didn't expect to live as long as they have done. When they were young, medicine wasn't as advanced as it is now, and many people died at an early age. Now we can expect to live into our 70s, and it is not impossible that within a few decades our life expectations will have increased even further. If this happens, the pressure on pension funds will be greater than ever – where will the money come from to support all the retired people?

The answer is clear – the money must primarily come from the people themselves, in the form of saving for retirement during their working lives. This is the reason for the trend towards money purchase schemes in general, and personal plans in particular, because these schemes are primarily funded by the people who join them.

Even if we didn't have an ageing population, pensions would still be complicated. There have to be strong laws and regulations to make sure that pension schemes and plans are properly run. Three other important factors increase the complexity:

● The ageing population is forcing the government to adjust the rules, and many of the changes must be phased in over many years – this makes things complicated. In the future, there may be more changes. For instance, the government might make it compulsory for everyone to join a pension scheme.
● Larger companies are reorganising their businesses to take advantage of information technology; this involves an increased use of 'outsourcing', which means giving internal work to outside contractors. More people will be working on short-term contracts, and will need personal pension plans.
● The pensions industry benefits from complications. You have to read books and pay advisers just to protect yourself from making a bad bargain – and every change in the rules can lead to some people paying too much in commissions and charges.

You still have some freedom, though. You are free to do virtually nothing, for instance. If you make no pension provision, you will still probably get a partial basic state pension, or some other state benefit. It won't be a great amount – but if you die before retirement age, it won't matter very much. Few people would say that this is a sensible choice.

Fortunately, you have other choices too. As well as, or instead of, contributing to a pension fund, you can save for your retirement in other ways. In order to make sure that your savings grow adequately, you will need to invest them wisely. In the rest of this chapter we will examine some ways of doing this.

── Investment and risk ──

The first thing to realise about any investment is that it is always risky to some degree; since no one can predict the future with complete accuracy, you cannot say that an investment has 0 per cent risk. If the world blows up tomorrow, all investments will be worthless.

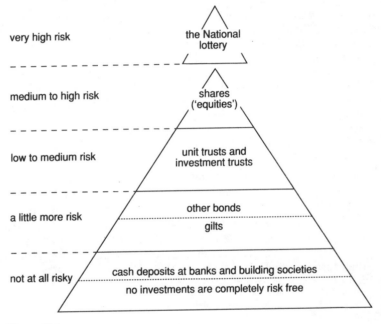

Figure 10.1

While you can't measure the degree of risk on an investment exactly, you can make a reasonable guess. Here is a list of common investments, in order of increasing risk.

- *Bank and building society deposits*
  These are generally thought of as being very low risk, because UK bank deposits of up to £20,000 pounds are protected by a deposit protection fund which will pay you 75 per cent of the value of the deposit if the bank goes bust. Building society deposits are protected to 90 per cent of the first £20,000 pounds (double this if you have a joint account).

● *Gilts*
'Gilts' or 'gilt-edged securities' are bonds issued by the British government; they get their name from their reputation for a high degree of safety. It is thought, justifiably, that if you lend the British government money by buying gilts, it is extremely unlikely that it will default on the loan. The British government has issued gilts for hundreds of years without ever having failed to meet payments on the due dates.

● *Other bonds*
A bond is an IOU issued by a government, local authority or a company in return for a loan of cash. A fixed rate of interest is payable to the bond holder, and the bond issuer promises to pay back the amount borrowed (the face value of the bond) at a certain time in the future. In the United Kingdom bonds are traditionally called 'stocks'.

● *Unit trusts and investment trusts*
These are funds of money that are invested in a wide range of assets by professionals.

● *Equities*
This is another name for shares. The risk of shares varies widely, but here we are talking about shares in companies that are quoted on the stock exchange.

Indirectly, you have already invested in some of these assets if you have a pension scheme or plan, because this is where much of the pension money goes.

TESSAs

If you are within a few years of retirement age, you probably won't want to expose your savings to much risk, especially if you are in a pension scheme where you can't change the date on which you retire.

Example

Joe had planned to retire at the end of 1987. In October 1987 the stock market crashed, reducing the value of his personal plan. He decided to postpone his retirement for several years in hope that the value of his fund would recover – fortunately for him, it did, so the gamble paid off.

To reduce your exposure to risk, it makes sense to put money into cash-based deposits, and TESSAs are a tax advantaged way of doing this.

Banks, building societies and incorporated friendly societies can offer TESSAs. These were launched in 1991 for everyone over 18. Married couples can each have a separate TESSA. If you keep to the rules, the interest on the account is free of tax, but if you break the rules, the interest will suffer tax at the investor's highest rate for the fiscal year in which the breach of the rules occurs.

When TESSAs first became available, they had enormous appeal because most interest rates offered a real return above inflation, and TESSAs offered an exceptional return. By late 1993, the fall in interest rates generally meant that even TESSAs were being closed in order for capital to be moved into risk investments with potential for higher growth.

TESSA rules

The main rule is that the capital deposited must not be withdrawn for five years. The net interest can be withdrawn without penalty during the five-year period. If you withdraw more than the net interest, the account loses its tax-free status. Thus, if the basic rate of tax is 25 per cent, a TESSA holder cannot withdraw more than 75 per cent of the interest from the account without breaking the rule.

The maximum amount that can be invested in a TESSA over five years is £9,000. Up to £150 can be invested on a regular monthly basis, or deposits can be of irregular amounts to suit the saver's convenience. However, not more than £3,000 may be invested in the first year and not more than £1,800 in each of the other four years. An investor who deposits less than the maximum amount in any one year cannot make up that amount by exceeding the the maximum in future years. Most providers set a minimum deposit, but this can be as low as £1.

TESSAs usually pay much more attractive interest rates than normal bank and building society rates for the same amount of capital. However, the interest rate is variable. After five years, the TESSA matures and loses its tax-free status. The investor can either with-draw the total investment tax free, or leave the money in the account, where whatever interest the provider pays thereafter will be liable to income tax at the investor's highest tax rate(s).

When the TESSA matures

When the TESSA matures, the investor is allowed to replace it by a new TESSA with its own five-year term. Originally, the rules for the second TESSA were identical to those for the first. For example, the maximum deposit in the first year would be £3,000 and the total invested over the whole of the second five-year period £9,000.

However, the danger of large capital outflows from building societies when the first TESSAs matured in 1996 was such that these rules were changed in the November 1994 budget. As the TESSAs mature, investors will be allowed to transfer all the capital they invested in their first TESSA into a new one, but they will not be allowed to transfer the interest earned on the first TESSA into the second. Thus, people who invested the maximum amount in their first TESSA will be able to open a new TESSA with £9,000 instead of £3,000. However, they will not be able to deposit additional amounts into their TESSA over the next five years.

People who invested less than £9,000 in their original TESSA will be able to add to their initial deposit over the next five years until the maximum allowed for each stage under the rules is reached. None of the foregoing applies to people who are investing in TESSAs for the first time.

Transferring a TESSA

Deposits can be transferred from one provider's TESSA to another with higher interest rates. Some providers charge a penalty for transfer, examples of which include a flat fee of £25, a loss of one month's inter-est or a loss of 90 days' interest. Such penalties are often associated with above average TESSA interest rates.

'Feeder' accounts

Many providers will open separate accounts for up to the £9,000 max-imum investment. This account will earn interest at normal (taxed) rates, and 'drip feed' money into the TESSA on the due dates for each annual instalment. Transfer of a TESSA is much more likely to attract a penalty when associated with a feeder account.

—— Personal Equity Plans (PEPs) ——

If you are younger, it makes sense to consider investing in the stock market. Although the value of such investments can go down as well as up, in the medium to long term (ten years or longer) stock market investments tend to perform better than other types of investment.

Personal Equity Plans (PEPs) are a tax-advantaged way of investing in the stock market. If you do not pay any tax in the United Kingdom and do not expect to in the future you can skip this section; PEPs are a tax break for British taxpayers designed to encourage wider share ownership.

To emphasise the point – please note that if you are a British resident but are not liable for tax (for instance, if you have a low income), then you should stay out of PEPs; astonishingly, there have been several cases recently of financial advisers putting non-taxpayers into PEPs.

When PEPs were introduced in 1986, they got off to a slow start, partly due to very complicated rules which required a lot of administration and provoked resistance to the scheme in the City of London. Since then, the restrictions and administrative burden on PEPs have been reduced, and they are now an attractive proposition to UK taxpayers.

The background

In the 1950s, the majority of shares in the United Kingdom were held by private investors. After two decades of social and political change, many private investors dropped out of the stock market, and new generations of people grew up who never considered the possibility of owning shares.

Important factors causing this decline were Capital Gains Tax (CGT) on shares (which initially taxed gains from inflation as well as 'real' gains), an investment income surcharge and the increase of tax breaks for house mortgages, pensions and insurance schemes. Private

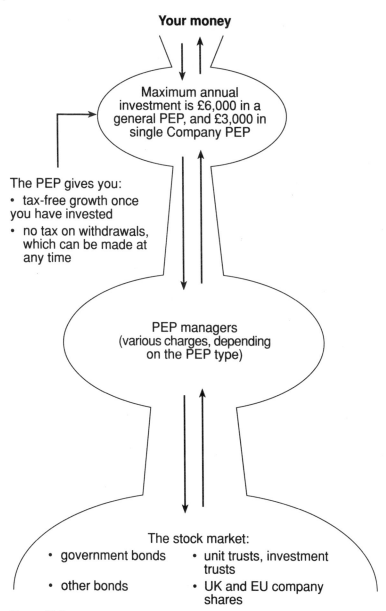

Your money

Maximum annual investment is £6,000 in a general PEP, and £3,000 in single Company PEP

The PEP gives you:
- tax-free growth once you have invested
- no tax on withdrawals, which can be made at any time

PEP managers (various charges, depending on the PEP type)

The stock market:
- government bonds
- other bonds
- unit trusts, investment trusts
- UK and EU company shares

Figure 10.2

individuals' money was still ending up on the stock market, but as part of the huge institutional funds which now began to dominate the City. By the late 1970s, small private investors had difficulty in finding a broker to act for them – the only real chance they had of owning shares was through unit trusts.

Another reason for the decline of the private investor was a decline in confidence, particularly during the industrial unrest of the 1970s, when restrictions on movement of money overseas, the oil crisis and labour problems combined to make the private investor feel that only unit trusts were safe investment vehicles.

With the advent of Thatcherism in 1979, the tide turned. The investment income surcharge was abolished, and CGT was indexed to take inflation into account. Tax breaks on life assurance were abolished, making this alternative less attractive. Slowly, industries that had been nationalised during the socialist reforms following the Second World War were 'privatised', having their shares sold to the public at a substantial discount. Finally, after the Big Bang and the introduction of PEPs, a new era for private shareholders began.

The way PEPs work

Anyone who is resident in the United Kingdom and over 18 may invest in a PEP. The PEP has to be managed by a person who is authorised to do so under the Financial Services Act. Currently, you can invest up to £6,000 a year in a 'General' PEP and up to a further £3,000 a year in a 'Single Company' PEP. Thus, a married couple can invest up to £18,000 per annum in PEPs, which is a substantial sum for most UK wage earners.

PEPs are free of tax on their dividends, and there is no CGT to pay on profits made from selling shares. Money held on deposit within a PEP is exempt from tax on the interest it earns, as long as the money is used to buy securities later.

Although PEP dividends are tax free, 20 per cent of their value is paid to the Inland Revenue by the PEP manager, who subsequently reclaims the money on behalf of the investors and returns it to their PEP accounts. This is an administrative advantage which is sometimes overlooked – small investors can avoid a large amount of paperwork by investing through a PEP.

Following a relaxation of the PEP rules, investors may cash in their PEPs at any time and still retain their tax breaks; some managers make a charge for early withdrawal, but this is still far less than the equivalent charges for early surrender of such things as endowment policies.

You don't have to put a lump sum into a PEP – you can make a monthly payment into a scheme. The only restriction is that you cannot make regular payments into more than one scheme at a time.

There are a variety of PEPs on offer:

Self-select PEPs
In this kind of scheme, an investor decides how the money is invested; the manager of the plan takes a small fee, and executes the investor's trading instructions without giving advice.

Advisory PEPs
A little more expensive than self-select PEPs, these are where the plan manager does give some advice on investments. Often these schemes are available only to a broker's well-established clients.

Managed or discretionary PEPs
This is where the investment decisions are made by the plan manager, not the individual.

Corporate PEPs
These usually are for shares in one company, and are most often used as part of an incentive scheme for employees of that company.

Single Company PEPs
These are restricted to shares in one company, with fewer restrictions than Corporate PEPs. They are useful to investors who have already invested the annual maximum of £6,000 in a General PEP, and wish to invest up to £3,000 more.

Unit trust and investment trust PEPs
These PEPs invest exclusively in unit trusts or investment trusts from a list chosen by the plan manager. Managed and self-select plans are available.

More on the tax advantages

The two big advantages of PEPs for the private investor are:

1 A big reduction in costly and time-consuming paperwork
2 The tax concessions.

Despite reductions, income tax is still a substantial burden for British residents, particularly those who pay the higher rate of 40 per cent. Those paying tax at the basic or lower rate may find that the tax saving is small in the early years after the deduction of set-up charges, say £20, and annual management fees, say 1 per cent, but if the value of the investment grows, the savings will too.

Capital Gains Tax is levied on gains in one year over a certain figure, currently £5,800. The rates of tax are constantly changing, and although CGT is now indexed against the Retail Price Index (RPI), it is difficult to calculate how much the CGT will be if you sell a particular investment. Capital losses can be set off against future gains.

Since PEPs are exempt from CGT, they are clearly essential for any investor who already pays CGT. Those who do not currently pay CGT may have their savings sunk into other CGT-exempt vehicles, such as their own homes, pensions schemes, gilts and insurance policies. PEPs offer you a chance to invest in the stock market while still enjoying CGT exemption.

PEP rules in more detail

Despite the increased flexibility of PEPs, you should be aware of the following restrictions.

Maximum allowances

As already mentioned, the maximum annual investments allowed are £6,000 into a General PEP and £3,000 into a Single Company PEP. Generally, PEP managers charge their fees on top, so the whole £9,000 can be invested. There are no minimum limits, but you probably won't find a manager who will let you invest less than £50 a month, except for unit trust and corporate PEPs. The annual allowances cannot be taken forward into future years, so, for example, if you invest only £8,000 in one year, you cannot bring forward the unused £1,000 of the allowance to the following year and add it to the £9,000 allowance for that year.

Another point to remember is that if you want to make up your allowances towards the end of a financial year (which ends on 5 April), you need to invest at least a fortnight before the year end to give PEP managers time to do the necessary paperwork for setting up, or topping up, the PEP.

Cash deposits with a PEP

Self-select PEP holders can hold cash deposits within a PEP and buy and sell shares at any time. Deposits must be held in designated sterling deposit accounts, which pay interest gross of tax. Any cash held on deposit must eventually be used to buy securities. An investor wanting tax breaks on permanent cash deposits should use the TESSA scheme.

Investment trusts and unit trusts

General PEPs may invest in 'qualifying' unit trusts and investment trusts. To qualify, the trusts must have at least 50 per cent of their total funds invested in ordinary shares of UK or EC companies quoted on a stock market. Additionally, up to £1,500 of the £6,000 allowance may be invested in 'non-qualifying' trusts who invest elsewhere in the world, and these must have more than 50 per cent in quoted ordinary shares.

Ordinary shares

Apart from the rules for unit and investment trusts, PEPs can be invested in the quoted ordinary shares of UK and EU countries. UK shares must be listed on the London Stock Exchange or traded on the Unlisted Securities Market.

Bonds

PEP funds can be invested in fixed-interest investments such as gilts or company bonds, as long as they are:

● denominated in sterling
● last for five years or more
● are issued by an organisation based in the EU.

Changing from one PEP manager to another

You can move a PEP from one manager to another at any time, but you may incur charges. Some managers make no charge at all, while others make a small charge of £20 to £30. Always check on the penalties, though, since a few managers make high charges for early withdrawal to 'lock in' their clients.

Some managers make a small charge for incoming PEPs, while most charge nothing. Occasionally, discounts are offered for incoming PEPs.

Note that some managers do limit the number of investments within a PEP, or have a minimum amount for any particular holding.

The ease of transfer and withdrawal is probably the most attractive feature of the PEP scheme. It helps investors to protect themselves against their PEP managers, and to take advantage of opportunities as they arise.

PEP dividends are tax free

Investors can withdraw their dividends tax free. Many plan managers distribute dividends every six months or annually, and investors in self-select PEPs can usually retrieve dividends sooner. Alternatively, you can leave the dividends in the fund to benefit from further growth and compound interest.

Putting existing share holdings into a PEP

You are allowed to transfer shares and unit trusts into a PEP, and various managers offer good terms for doing so.

Cashing in your PEP

You can cash in all or part of a PEP at any time, exempt of tax. What you can't do, is to withdraw cash from a PEP and then reinvest it in a PEP in the same year. Check plan managers' penalties for partial withdrawal or early withdrawal, and avoid those with high charges.

How to choose a PEP

There are hundreds of PEPs on the market, managed by over 200 different managers. The variety of schemes available can be confusing, so the first thing to do is to ask yourself the following questions:

Do I want freedom to choose or professional management?
The truly passive investor can use a unit/investment trust PEP or a managed PEP, while others may prefer a self-select PEP. Confident investors should choose the latter, since the charges are lower, you can minimise your risk by investing in a spread of lower risk ('blue

chip') shares, and you have the freedom to take advantage of the opportunities you find.

Do I want growth or income?

It's probably best to look for funds which offer a better-than-average income and are mainly invested in shares, since these have a chance for good capital growth, rather than the funds which offer the highest income rates, since these will have restricted growth potential, having up to half of their portfolios in fixed-interest securities.

Should I diversify or concentrate my portfolio?

It depends on what proportion your PEP funds take up of your available funds for investment. If they are a small part, say less than 30 per cent, you can afford to concentrate on particular shares, perhaps even through a corporate PEP, which has very low charges, while diversifying your other investments elsewhere. Conversely, if your PEPs are a large part of your total investments, make sure they are well diversified, into at least 15 shares across a range of countries and industries.

What kind of manager do I want?

You definitely don't want managers who reluctantly offer PEPs, either to keep existing clients, or because they want to offer a complete range of services. Choose your manager carefully, and remember that you can always switch to another manager if you are not satisfied. Many brokers, banks, building societies, insurance companies, solicitors and financial advisers manage PEPs – pick one who will give good service and reasonable charges.

Managed PEPs

Managed PEPs advise clients to keep their portfolio to between 10 and 20 shares, which is low for adequate diversification. There are four types of scheme.

- *Just shares*
  Some managed PEPs invest only in shares; these do not offer enough diversification, and tend to have high charges. Possibly worthwhile for larger investors are the share-only schemes which have good portfolios and low charges.

- *Share and investment trusts*
  These invest in investment trusts as well as shares, offering wider diversification. You may be able to choose your trusts, but usually from a limited number offered by the manager.

- *Share and unit trusts*
  These combine unit trusts with shares, and operate like the previous scheme.

- *Combinations*
  These are schemes which invest in unit trusts, investment trusts and shares; usually, they do not allow the investor any freedom of selection.

Unit and investment trust PEPs

It's easy to get confused between managed PEPs which mix investments between shares and/or unit and investment trusts, and another PEP category of unit and investment trust PEPs which invest exclusively in unit and investment trusts. For an investor who really wants a professional manager to make the decisions, they are probably the most suitable form of PEP, being less restrictive than managed PEPs.

Unit trusts

More popular than investment trusts, their 'front-end' management charges can be steep. Though often quoted at around 6 per cent, these charges can be as high as 9.5 per cent depending on demand, so timing is important.

The bid/offer spread is the price difference between that at which the manager will buy, or 'bid', for units, and the price at which he will sell, or 'offer', them to you. To make a profit from unit trusts, your units have to grow more than the bid/offer spread.

You can opt for the power to select your own trusts from a list provided by the manager; if you want to do this, it is better to choose a PEP which is managed by a large group which offers a wide range of trusts to choose from. You should also check whether you are charged for switching between trusts, or whether you can do so at a discount (up to 5 per cent). Check whether the manager lets you hold more than one trust at a time within a PEP.

Most managers do not charge management fees on top of the already high unit trust fees, or offer a discount on the trusts to balance their fees. There is often a penalty for withdrawing funds in the first two or three years.

Investment trusts

These are less common than unit trust schemes, and, like them, you can find schemes which let you choose the trusts from a list provided by the manager.

Initial charges can be as high as 4 per cent, which makes such schemes uncompetitive, but some make very low charges.

Unit and investment trust schemes

These are less common, but operate in a similar way.

Which one to choose?

Unit trusts invest in a large number of shares, carefully diversified. The price of a unit to an investor is found by dividing the value of the trust's portfolio by the number of units already issued, after taking into account the 'bid/offer spread' of about 6 per cent. This spread includes initial charges and dealing costs, but there is usually an annual charge of around 1.5 per cent in addition; this charge is taken out of dividends paid to the investor.

Investment trusts are actually limited companies which invest in shares and other securities. The trust's own shares are quoted on the stock exchange and can sometimes be bought at a discount to the value of the trust's portfolio – they are thus more volatile than unit trusts, but can do better. There are no initial charges, and the annual management fee should be about 0.5 per cent.

Generally speaking, investment trusts are better value than unit trusts. Unit trusts are better known because they are more widely marketed.

Self-select PEPs

This is the PEP option that gives you the most freedom. You can invest in any share quoted in London and many others quoted in continental Europe. You can mix shares with trusts, or stick completely to trusts. Managers give no advice, and should make very low charges.

Watch out for dealing charges; 1.25 to 1.5 per cent (plus VAT) is average, and they can be much lower. If they are very low, check the manager's charging system for higher charges elsewhere. Most managers charge £20 or less as a minimum commission on dealing – don't accept a higher rate than this.

What you can't do

Some self-select PEPs make you choose shares from a limited number, often the shares in the FTSE 100 index. Others give you a limit on the number of different shares you can hold within a single PEP. If you will be investing in PEPs for several years, this second restriction is not necessarily harsh, since you can build a well-diversified portfolio over a few years by investing in combinations of different shares each year.

Watch out for management charges for sending you company reports or attending meetings; they should be free. You should avoid 'dividend collection fees', levied each time you receive a dividend into your PEP.

Advisory PEPs

The main difference between advisory PEPs and self-select PEPs is that advisory PEP managers do give advice on trading in shares, as well as on more general matters such as financial planning. They are hard to find, and are usually run by small stockbrokers in the provinces. Minimum commissions can be high. Small brokers can offer a good personal service, but they need clients who either trade frequently or who invest large amounts.

Single Company PEPs

Single Company PEPs have a £3,000 annual limit, and are intended for investors who have already invested £6,000 in a General PEP. They can be run by a different manager, but you may find that your General PEP manager offers no initial charges and other inducements to encourage you to remain loyal.

You must invest in the shares of only one company at any one time, but you are allowed to switch to another share as often as you wish. If you sell the shares, you must reinvest the money within 42 days, which means that even if the market as a whole is going bad, you cannot stay out of it for long. There is no point in using a Single Company PEP if you have £6,000 or less to invest in a particular year – you get more flexibility in a self-select PEP.

Summary

The tax advantages of a PEP is a possible, although riskier, alternative to a pension scheme or plan. If you invest the maximum allowed each year for 30 years or so, the fund should grow to quite a respectable size by the time you retire, and when you retire, you don't have to buy an annuity unless you want to. As always, get professional advice before taking the plunge!

GLOSSARY

accrual rate in the final salary schemes, this is the annual rate at which you build up your pension. For example, if the rate is $\frac{1}{60}$, your pension builds up at $\frac{1}{60}$ of your final salary for each year you are in the scheme

accrued benefits also known as 'accrued rights', these are the benefits which have already built up at any particular time

actuary an expert who calculates statistical probabilities; the pension and insurance industries use them extensively

added years in final salary schemes, some AVCs let you top up your main scheme by building up extra benefits, calculated as notional added years to the scheme

Additional Voluntary Contributions (AVCs) separate funds to which you can make extra contributions, over and above your normal contributions to an occupational scheme; the maximum total contributions to both schemes is 15 per cent of your earnings each year

annuitant a person who buys an annuity (see below)

annuity to obtain a pension from a money purchase pension, you must buy an annuity on retirement. In exchange for your pension funds, an insurance company guarantees to pay you a regular pension, either for life or for a fixed number of years. When you die, the pension stops and the insurance company keeps the funds

annuity rate Annuities are essentially fixed-interest investments, although there can be some variation in the annuity rate over time. The rate is the percentage of the pension fund that the insurance company will pay you back each year

appropriate personal pension (APP) These are personal pensions specifically for contracting out of SERPs

band earnings   your earnings between the 'lower earnings limit' (LEL) and the 'upper earnings limit' (UEL); they are used to calculate certain National Insurance contributions

basic state pension   also known as the old age pension, this is a small pension paid by the state and is based on your National Insurance contributions record. Many people do not qualify for the full pension

benefits   word used by the DSS to mean the welfare payments it makes, and by the pensions industry to mean any money paid to you, your spouse or your dependants by a pension scheme or plan

bid/offer spread   with unit-linked plans and unit trusts, this is a charge you pay when you purchase units. It is expressed as the difference ('spread') between the price at which you can buy units (the 'bid') and the price at which you could immediately sell them (the 'offer')

capital levy/capital units   type of charge in unit-linked plans, used to pay commissions. To be avoided if possible

commutation   the act of taking part of your pension as a tax-free lump sum

COMPS   a contracted-out money purchase scheme

contracted in   refers to individual employees or company schemes that remain in SERPS

contracted out   refers to opting out of SERPS, either by individual employees or company schemes. Most schemes are contracted out

contributions   the money that you or your employer pays into your pension scheme or plan. National Insurance contributions are different – they are a tax, but are used to calculate state pension entitlements

Death in Retirement benefit   pension paid to your spouse or dependants if you die after you retire

Death is Service benefit   pension paid to your spouse or dependants if you die while you are still employed

Department of Social Security (DSS)   government department which administers state benefits, collects National Insurance and pays state pensions. Heavily bureaucratic and often overstretched, it can be difficult to deal with – always be polite and patient and put and ask for everything in writing

dependant   someone whom you are supporting financially – usually your spouse or children under 18, but some schemes accept unmarried partners as dependants potentially eligible for benefits

discretionary benefits   benefits that some pension schemes may pay you, but are not guaranteed. For example, you may have a guaranteed minimum pension and a discretionary bonus on top, depending on the investment performance of a fund

employer pension schemes another name for occupational schemes, they are only open to employees

executive pension plan (EPP) an advantageous occupational scheme for company executives

final salary scheme an occupational scheme where your pension and other benefits are linked to your 'final salary' in the year before you retire. In practice, the final salary calculation may be based on an average of several years' salaries

Free Standing Additional Voluntary Contributions (FSAVCs) a top-up scheme for employees who otherwise will not receive the maximum pension from a final salary scheme. FSAVCs are run by insurance companies

Funded Unapproved Schemes (FURBS) these schemes are recognised by the Inland Revenue but do not enjoy the normal tax benefits of pension schemes. They are used by higher-earning employees to provide extra pension money in retirement – the pension is taxed as a 'benefit in kind'

gilts a shortened name for 'gilt-edged securities', which are bonds issued by the UK government. By buying a bond you are lending money to the government in return for interest payments

guaranteed minimum pension (GMP) the minimum amount of pension you will get from a final salary scheme in respect of periods when you were contracted out of SERPS

Home Responsibilities Protection (HRP) a scheme designed to protect your state pensions when you are looking after someone at home – such as a child or an elderly person

hybrid schemes occupational pension schemes which combine elements of final salary schemes and money purchase schemes

inflation the increase in prices – in other words, a reduction in the buying power of cash. It is caused by many factors, and is impossible to measure precisely, but one approximate measurement is the Retail Prices Index (RPI) published by the government

Inland Revenue government department which collects most taxes, including income tax

insured schemes pension schemes run by insurance companies

life office a life assurance company or part of an insurance company that sells life assurance and pensions products

lower earnings limit (LEL) the lower limit on your earnings at which National Insurance is payable. It is used by the DSS to calculate various benefits

married women's reduced-rate contributions a lower rate of Class 1 National Insurance which some married women and widows pay. The contributions do not build up full rights to state pensions

middle-band earnings the same as 'band earnings' (see page 151)

money purchase scheme a scheme where you get your pension by buying an annuity when you retire. Personal pension plans are money purchase schemes

mutual life office a life office which is technically owned by the people who buy its polices. It is not a company with shareholders

National Insurance a tax on earnings used to calculate state pensions

National Insurance rebate a proportion of National Insurance contributions which the DSS pays in to a personal pension plan if you contract out of SERPS into an 'appropriate pension plan' (APP)

net relevant earnings if you are an employee, these are approximately your gross earnings, and if you are self-employed they are your net profits. They are used to calculate how much you can legally contribute to a personal pension plan.

occupational pension scheme a pension scheme for employees – final salary schemes and money purchase schemes are both occupational pension schemes

pensionable earnings in occupational schemes, these are the part of your earnings on which your contributions to the main scheme are based

pensioneer trustee an independent trustee who must be one of the trustees of a small self-administered scheme (SSAS)

performance in pensions, and investment generally, the word means how well or badly a fund has grown during the time it has been invested. You can only know how well a fund has 'performed' in hindsight

Personal Equity Plan (PEP) a scheme for investing in the stock market which gives tax incentives to UK taxpayers. The rules have been relaxed over the past few years, making PEPs increasingly attractive, but this could change in the future

personal pension plan a money purchase scheme for people who are not members of an occupational scheme. See 'appropriate personal pensions'

plan provider an organisation which runs a personal pension plan

preserved pension the pension you receive from a pension scheme or plan to which you are no longer contributing

purchased life annuity (PLA) an annuity which you buy with your tax-free lump sum or other money rather than with the balance of a pension fund

qualifying year a DSS definition of a year's National Insurance contributions or credits which count towards your basic state pension

reduction in premium (RIP) a way of expressing the effect of charges on your pension investment, it shows the percentage of your premiums which are taken in charges

Reduction in yield (RIY) a way of expressing the effect of changes on your pension investment, it shows how much the annual growth of the fund is reduced by charges

Retail Prices Index (RPI) a government measurement of the average level of retail prices in the United Kingdom. The annual change in the RPI is a way of approximating annual inflation

Retirement Pension Forecasting and Advice Service DSS service for telling you what are your current and forecast entitlements to state pensions. This is the best practical way of working out your entitlement, and you are allowed one forecast a year for free

self-invested personal pensions (SIPPS) a type of personal plan where you have more control over how the fund is invested. Can be suitable if you are a high earner and have some investment experience

small self-administered scheme (SSAS) a type of occupational pension scheme for controlling directors of companies, giving special benefits including some freedom to use the pension fund to invest in the company itself

State Earnings Related Pension Scheme (SERPS) an earnings related state pension scheme for employees, based on National Insurance contributions. You can choose to stay in SERPS or to contract out into an occupational scheme or an 'appropriate personal pension'.

stock in the United Kingdom, the word is traditionally used to describe fixed-interest investments, otherwise known as 'bonds'. In the USA, a 'stock' means a share in a company. This can cause confusion, since more and more people in the UK are adopting the American usage to refer to certain types of share transactions

transfer analysis if you are considering making a transfer, you should ask an adviser for a transfer analysis to make sure that it is worthwhile transferring

transfer value the lump sum you take out of a pension scheme to transfer it to another scheme or plan

trust a special legal form of ownership used with many occupational pension schemes to separate the pension money from the rest of the company's money

trustee a person who looks after money held in trust. Trustees have heavy legal obligations to do their job properly, but you don't have to be a professional to become one. If you are a member of a pension scheme, it may be possible to become a trustee of the funds

unit trusts a type of investment fund where your investment is pooled with those of other investors, and you buy and sell 'units' in the fund – their price changes in line with the performance of the fund, so they can go down as well as up

unitised with-profits plan a type of pension plan run by some insurance companies where your pension contributions are linked to units in a similar way to unit trusts (see unit trusts) but are more complicated and may have hidden charges

upper earnings limit (UEL) the maximum level of your earnings on which you must pay National Insurance contributions

with-profits plan A type of pension plan offered by insurance companies. The value of your pension depends on how well the insurance company performs, but it gives you a guaranteed minimum pension fund when it matures, with possible extra bonuses. Charges can be high

working life a DSS definition used to work out how much basic state pension will get.

FURTHER INFORMATION

Useful addresses

Association of British Insurers
51 Gresham Street
London EC2V 7HQ
Tel: 0171 600 3333

Association of Consulting Actuaries
1 Wardrobe Place
London EC4V 5AH
Tel: 0171 248 3163

Association of Pension Lawyers (APL)
c/o Travers Smith Braithwaite
10 Snow Hill
London EC1A 2AL
Tel: 0171 248 9133

Association of Pensioneer Trustees
c/o J B Trustees
20 Bank Street
Lutterworth
Leicestershire LE17 4AG
Tel: 01455 559711

Chartered Association of Certified Accountants (ACCA)
29 Lincoln's Inn Fields
London WC2A 3EE
Tel: 0171 396 5800

Financial Intermediaries, Managers and Brokers Regulatory
Association (FIMBRA)
Hertsmere House
Hertsmere Road
London E14 4AB
Tel: 0171 538 8860

Inland Revenue (Savings and Investment Division)
South West Wing
Bush Street
London WC2RB 4RD
Tel: 0171 438 6622

Insurance Ombudsman
City Gate One
135 Park Street
London SE1 9EA
Tel: 0171 401 8700

Investment Management Regulatory Organisation (IMRO)
Broadwalk House
5 Appold House
London EC2A 2LL
Tel: 0171 628 6022

Life Assurance and Unit Trust Regulatory Organisation (LAUTRO)
Centre Point
103 New Oxford Street
London WC1A 1QH
Tel: 0171 379 0444

National Association of Pension Funds (NAPF)
12–18 Grosvenor Gardens
London SW1W 0DH
Tel: 0171 730 0585

Occupational Pensions Advisory Service (OPAS)
11 Belgrave Road
London SW1V 1RB
Tel: 0171 233 8080

Pensions Ombudsman
11 Belgrave Road
London SW1V 1RB

Personal Investment Authority (PIA)
3–4 Royal Exchange
London EC3V 3NL
Tel: 0171 929 0072

PIA Ombudsman
1 London Wall
London EC2Y 5EA
Tel: 0171 600 4727

Pre-Retirement Association
Nodus Centre
University Campus
Guildford
Surrey GU2 5RX
Tel: 01483 259747

Registrar of Pension Schemes
Occupational Pensions Board
PO Box 1NN
Newcastle-upon-Tyne NE99 1NN
Tel: 0191 225 6394

Securities and Investment Board (SIB)
Gavrelle House
2–14 Bunhill Row
London EC1Y 8RA
Tel: 0171 638 1240

Society of Pension Consultants (SPC)
Ludgate House
Ludgate Circus
London EC4A 2AB
Tel: 0171 353 1688

Magazines

Money Management
Tel: 0171 405 6969

Occupational Pensions
Tel: 0171 354 5858

Pensions Management
Tel: 0181 402 8485

Pensions World
Tel: 0181 686 9141

Planned Savings
Tel: 0181 868 4499

INDEX